W9-AUC-317

THE
LIVING CODE

(TLC)

Deciphering Life's Spiritual Messages by Learning to Live From the Heart

Linda and Brenda McCoy

Twin Heart Productions
Springfield, Missouri

The Living Code

Decipher Life's Spiritual Messages by
Learning to Live From the Heart

Copyright © 2009 Linda McCoy, Brenda McCoy
First Edition – December, 2009

Cover design and Text layout by Dave Lappin
Editing by Katie Ann Hillelson
Final editing by "The Twins" and our Angels/Spiritual Guides

All rights reserved. This book may not be reproduced in whole or in part, or transmitted in any form, without written permission from the authors. Nor may any part of this book be reproduced, stored in a retrieval system, or transmitted in any form or by any means electronic, mechanical, photocopying, recording, or other, without written permission from the authors.

As with any outside information, the information presented here should be viewed as seed material for contemplation only. The authors do not dispense medical advice nor prescribe "medical treatment" for physical, mental, or emotional imbalances.

The information in this book is our truth only, and not meant to be taken as your truth or the "ultimate truth." Life has taught us that truth is relative according to our belief system. Anything stated in this book could change as we continue on our spiritual path.

ISBN 978-0-9842839-0-3
Library of Congress Control Number: 2009939314

Twin Heart Productions
P. O. Box 3182
Springfield, MO 65808

www.thelivingcode.com

Printed in the United States by
LightningSource™/Ingram Book Group

Note to the Reader

Please do not follow or use any meditation exercises given in this book while driving a vehicle or using equipment of any type. Use these exercises only in a safe, comfortable environment.

Acknowledgement

Thanks to the Holy Spirit and all our guides/angels in our inner writing room for helping us to bring heaven to earth.

Thanks to Tom and Dave, our wonderful husbands, for all their help. Thanks to Skip Lawton and Alana McCormick for use of their beautiful cottage in the woods in Branson, Missouri—www.thelightwithin.info.

Thank you to Brenda's husband, Dave, for his expertise in creating, from the heart, our beautiful cover design, page layout, and web site.

Thank you to our editor, Katie Ann Hillelson, who, through synchronistic events, came our way before we had thoughts of hiring an editor.

We also want to thank our proofreaders, Cynthia Rutledge, Janet Helms, and Dave Lappin. A special thank you to Tom Summer for that critical "last minute" proofreading into the wee hours of the night.

Another special thanks to Michael Harrington for his encouragement and valuable assistance through the publishing process, and to everyone, our teachers, that played their "exceptional parts" in our life "story" enabling us to master *The Living Code*.

Dedication

We dedicate this book to all the children born around the beginning of the new millennium who are helping us move into the new energy of the Aquarian Age. They are a bench mark for a period of spiritual awakening that is now occurring on the planet. This generation will be seeking deeper spiritual values that will create a more peaceful earth. These special children are here to lead us into new paradigms, giving birth to the new earth—strengthening our intuitive communication with the One Creator, by teaching us how to live from the heart.

Contents

Preface

The Living Code is a spiritual autobiography of the "twins—the real McCoy's." We share our life's journey from our fundamental Christian upbringing to our spiritual awakening, which happened through non-traditional experiences. These living experiences turned our personal and spiritual foundations upside down. We connected with a Higher Power/Holy Spirit, which put us on a path that was considered heresy to our church doctrine.

Many today are seeking something beyond their current religious teachings. We feel that many will be able to relate to our journey from being "religious" to being "spiritual," and our explanation of the difference.

In the spring of 2007, we began a discussion about co-authoring a book—possibly finishing the one started over ten years ago.

Brenda began pondering how to fit this into her busy schedule. What a relief when one morning in meditation, like a breath of fresh air to her over-scheduled mind, an intuitive flash said, "You only have to write one-half of a book. Both of you already have a lot of it written, and your little daily journal, *The Living Code,* is the perfect title."

To our relief and appreciation, Linda's schedule often permitted her more time to write the initial draft on many chapters, and then together we enjoyed the creative intuitive flow of joint-editing. Relieved, Brenda realized how easily her insights were seamlessly woven into what Linda had written, a confirmation of Spirit's guiding hand.

Our joint writing was a labor of love and excitement as our connection with Divine Spirit grew even stronger. We both knew that it was time to write the insights from our personal and joint stories and share our spiritual journey.

Even though we often felt vulnerable as we shared the personal stories, it was a risk we had to take. We knew this was our next spiritual step.

This book is meant to be read from the heart, which enables your pondering spirit to connect with the essence, the Spirit behind the written words, which takes you to a deeper level. Our writing style, as guided by Divine Spirit, is more the *intuitive way—free style*, if you will; we wrote what was placed in our hearts. *The Living Code*, as is life, will always be a work-in-progress.

We have always had a pondering spirit—asking questions of life and not even realizing, at first, what we were doing. Eventually, when the answers would appear so close to the time we asked the question, we began to catch on to the dynamics of the play of life. Putting our questions on the back burner to *ponder* became a way of life. Little did we know at the time that this would come to be a vital key in our spiritual communication process.

Throughout the book you will find *Ponderism* questions. The art of pondering serves to activate your natural intuitive ability to receive insightful and inspirational messages. Asking a question is an important component in learning the process of pondering, because this questioning creates a magnetic process—drawing to you the answer that is *truth* for you at that moment. Pondering something, the art of asking a question, serves to activate the Universal Law of Attraction—"ask and it is given."

Writing this book on the physical level has been a great learning experience in helping us move into a spiritual writing style. This means that we were taken away from the traditional way of writing—from the mind, to the intuitive way of writing—from the heart. Each time we came together to write, we would also join each other on an inner level, which we called our "inner writing room," to simultaneously write and co-edit with Divine Spirit.

In this room, we experienced many things and never knew what to expect, as periodically when we arrived, things had changed. It varied from the presence of our writing/editing guides and a room full of people one day, to showing up one morning to an empty room. Startled, we asked, "What was going on?" Suddenly, we saw the completed book on a reading stand— emitting a glowing white light. Then, for some time, the room was full of people reading the book. They shared it with others, and the fire of expansion was lit as they took it out into the world.

As the writing process progressed we needed to meet more often, so for many months we began a regular early-morning schedule via the telephone. Thankfully, it got easier when we changed to the Skype Internet program allowing us to talk via our computers. We were grateful for the new tech-savvy world of Skype, laptops, wireless, and e-mail. Our job was so much easier than when we first started to co-author a book in the mid-nineties.

When it came time for us to edit what we had written, we asked to see the final manuscript in our inner writing room. On the physical level, as we looked at the chapter we were editing on our computers, one of us would read it out loud, as if reading from the finished book in the inner writing room, and the other would be listening to the rhythm and flow of what was being said, while viewing a copy on the computer. On many occasions the one reading would say words that were not on the computer copy. This was our confirmation that the inner copy we were reading was, indeed, slightly different from the outer physical copy.

Anytime we couldn't seem to get it right, we would take a moment and reconnect to the writing room, and the creative flow would start again. Writing was such a joy in this manner, we seldom experienced writer's block because one of us always seemed to have the right words to keep the flow going.

Throughout the book we use symbols to define whose experience we are sharing: L ♫ or B ♫.

Notes from the Editor

When I begin editing a manuscript, intuitively I tune into the energy of the author(s) and the spirit of intent behind the words on the page. This gives me a deeper understanding of why and how the manuscript is being written. Because of this, Linda and Brenda have dubbed me their "Cosmic Editor." The experience of attuning to the spirit behind *The Living Code* was the most powerful of my career. I believe this is because the authors wrote with Divine Guidance from their Inner Writing Room. It was written from the heart, so you, the reader, are advised to read the book the same way—from your heart, not just with your mind. The result will be a multidimensional experience.

Perhaps a Warning Label should accompany this book: WARNING, READING THIS BOOK COULD CHANGE YOUR LIFE FOREVER! The process of editing brought up personal issues for me to examine and transform; things I thought I had worked through years ago. Nevertheless, it was a labor of love because I recognized the value of the twins having the courage to bare their souls in order to guide others in their spiritual growth. I have known them for a number of years and know that they always strive to "walk their talk," so I encourage you to place yourself in the role of student as you read. Not only do they share their experiences, they give you very powerful tools to deal with your own issues.

The section on Waking Dreams is especially pertinent to the busy lives that most of us live today. I have worked with this concept for many years, but during the editing process my focus in this area was heightened, and I had profound experiences of unusual guidance. The things we would ordinarily call coincidence, luck, an accident, a twist of fate, or chance can become waking dreams, and empower our decision making.

The twins share their experiences with asking for specific signs in outer life for Divine Guidance which is the process they share of learning to live from the heart—*The Living Code*. This is another, more structured way to read the signs of life to guide you in making decisions.

Whether you have been on a conscious spiritual path for many years or are just beginning, the tools presented here are timeless and have several levels of understanding. Because my own background and life experiences are similar to that of the twins, I can attest to how effectively they have transformed themselves spiritually, mentally, emotionally and even physically, while using the methods presented here. This is one thing that makes them powerfully effective teachers—they have lived it!

All three of us have lived through the still, small voice within leading us away from a mainstream Christian background into the unknown. We know the challenges and heartaches, the uncertainty and anxiety that come with turning away from the known and learning to trust the wonderful things you are discovering as a greater Truth. This book will show you that you do not have to throw away everything you believe, in order to find greater Truth.

It was a distinct honor and privilege to edit this writing. Love is the answer to any question—you will find many answers within these pages.

May You Walk in the Light,
Katie Ann Hillelson

Introduction

This book has been written in service to humanity, with a desire to help others remember and strengthen their intuitive nature, which is inherent in all of us. We share a practical user-friendly system that helped us enhance our connection and communication with our intuition, which we will refer to as the *Intuitive Guidance System*, or *IGS*. This system greatly accelerated our personal search for truth. Our terminology, throughout this book, when referring to the Intuitive Guidance System may include, but is not limited to: soul, intuition, Holy Spirit, angels, guides, God, or Source Energy.

This information is not new, as today many are already aware of their connection with their IGS. Our hope is that by reading this book, you might find more tools to enhance that connection. For some, this information will be a trip *back to the basics*—which is often helpful in taking us to a new level of spiritual awareness.

Life is alive with information, *The Living Code* (TLC); each moment is encoded with symbolic messages that can be read, deciphered, and utilized by those who know how. Some have considered this an "instruction manual" as a guide in their search for answers to life's many challenges and helpful in finding their soul's purpose.

Our life experiences are shared as examples to help others set up their own living code and, thus, have dialog directly with Spirit. Once the living code is set up, you will learn how to become the *watcher* of life rather than the *victim* of life. Then, the major crossroads in your life will become your friends instead of your foes.

"Watch out that you are not deceived." Luke 21:8

We are in times of great discernment. This book is about learning to trust your inner guidance by seeking your own confirmations within. If asked, the Spirit of discernment will join you on your journey through this book so that what cannot be proven, will be discerned as to whether it is truth for you. Anything less than your truth does not matter and the same is so for others. We do not claim to have anyone's *gospel truth*; truth-seeking is an inside job belonging to your IGS.

Our Story—The Journey

We were born in the late 1940's into a farming community in Southeast Missouri, near the Great Mississippi River. We were the last of nine children and the second set of twins; the other siblings ranged in ages from seven to twenty—this generation gap was to play a major role in our life experiences.

The day of our birth was remembered by many because a devastating tornado came through the town the next day. The family watched in horror as, on their way to visit the new siblings, they saw the tornado heading toward the vicinity of the hospital. The tornado had come within a few blocks of the hospital and, much to their relief, everyone was safe. Thus began our journey of life on Planet Earth.

Little did we know that the turbulence of this event would mirror much of our life's journey—becoming a catalyst in accelerating our process of learning to stay in the "eye of the storm." Life on the farm was about hard work and scarcity, but it gave us a value system we would later come to appreciate and rely on, helping us to weather the storms of life.

A principle focus of our upbringing was that we were not to question authority figures—especially the family fundamental religious beliefs. We were not raised in a family that openly showed their affections. Our parents were of the generation that did not give praise; criticism and guilt were the most productive ways to keep children in line, except for the whippings with the belt or the peach tree limb (those really smarted). It was really a bummer to have to cut your own switch; our mother firmly believed, "spare the rod and spoil the child."

Our strict religious teachings taught that we should "shun all appearance of evil," which included wearing shorts and bathing suits, swimming in public, playing with poker cards, and any functions that had dancing—our saving grace was that, at least, when we reached age sixteen, we could wear makeup.

We were identical twins who looked so much alike that our school teachers and some classmates couldn't tell us apart—even our mother had difficulty at times. One time when Linda was ill, it was Brenda who got the aspirin. On one occasion we switched classes in high school and the teacher never knew it.

Typically, we did not want to be separated. In discussing our childhood, our older sister commented that, as small children, when one of us left the room the other one soon followed. We dressed alike most of our childhood and had lots of fun with this in high school—sewing many of our own clothes. People were always comparing us with each other, trying to figure out who was who—this, for us, began the *comparison trap*. As we entered puberty we fell into this trap often, which brought many changes as we became competitive in dating, grades, and life in general. Not having grown up in an affectionate family, getting attention or acknowledgement from others—which we did easily as twins—became our misperception of feeling loved and, thus, valued.

The "dis-ease to please" settled into our belief system as we felt a great need to be responsible for other peoples' happiness, with self-sacrifice as a key component—a "woman's thing." We soon realized that when we pleased others, we felt valued and loved. Because this was a foreign feeling for us, it created a pattern of looking outside of ourselves for validation.

The need to receive attention or acknowledgement from others became an addiction, and as such, we could never get enough! Gaining attention as twins satisfied our addiction, but served to create a false sense of self-confidence. This made it difficult when we separated after high school because, with the separation, we no longer got attention, and this left us with a great sense of loss and a void in our heart that we didn't understand. The result was an identity crisis. It would be many years before we totally understood what was happening.

In school we tried to "fit in" and appear "normal," but it became a juggling act as our social life could only go so far because of our religious teachings. We were popular in school and always on the honor roll. Today, we realize that we were *right-brained*, intuitive children growing up in a *left-brained*, intellectual world, which enhanced our lack of self-confidence.

At eighteen we went our separate ways, moving to different states; Linda went to a Christian college and Brenda married. We had very little contact with each other until the age of thirty, when we finally reconnected after

Linda's divorce. We had a lot of fun marveling at the parallels in our personal relationships, spiritual insights, personal issues, and even our dreams. We would often call each other to recommend a book only to find the other already reading it.

We discovered that, individually, we were often learning the same Spiritual lessons but through different circumstances. We both opted out of traditional higher education and looking back at our life journey, we understood why. We were "home schooled by the Holy Spirit" and our life experiences became our school house of Higher Education. When we reconnected at age thirty, we began to notice something magical and mystical happening in our experiences. We soon discovered that our combined energies brought more clarity and insights into the experiences and dreams that we shared.

The fire of Divine Spirit had been lit, and life became an exciting adventure. We began to find, and understand, the *Living Code* woven into the very fabric of our daily experiences. This code had been there all along, just waiting to be deciphered by those willing to ask, seek, and be open to receive a new perspective. In our hearts we felt a truth surface that would bring a new understanding of ourselves, life, and God. Learning how to decipher life's secret code became our goal. Finally, help arrived to start the process of leveling out the *roller-coaster-ride* of life.

This book is about *our story* —the good, the bad, and the beautiful that served as a boot camp for our spiritual growth, and taught us that we are more than *our story*. The courage to share this information is our gift in service. We offer this book with the hope that others will learn how to ask the important life question—*what's beyond my story?* Since your story is not your True Self, when you become the Watcher of your life events, you can easily recognize who's on stage.

The Twins' Spiritual Dictionary

For clarity, we have given our definition of a few words that we will be using throughout the book. *The Living Code* is a "present moment" communication system; therefore, these definitions are subject to change.

God: Synonymous with: Divine Spirit, Source Energy, Higher Power, Holy Spirit, the Father–Oneness with the Eternal Presence.

Intuitive Guidance System (IGS): The authentic inner guidance that we receive from the soul. To have clear intuition, put yourself into a neutral state of mind when making a decision. This opens you to the intuitive level where clear intuition will bring to you the right solution at the right time.

Do not confuse the intuitive level with the level where disincarnate beings live the illusion of being teachers and the forces of chaos are active at this time. This is why the Christian Bible says, "try the spirits." Always have the intent to seek the highest spiritual level possible and if an inner message does not feel right or is detrimental in anyway, it is not coming from the Spirit of Truth. You can always ask for a confirmation. The true test is when you do not feel the need to announce to others where your guidance has come from unless specifically asked.

Soul: Soul has no form, movement, or location in the physical world, but it has the ability to know, see, hear, and perceive all things—past, present, future—often referred to as the "Higher Self." Soul is patiently waiting for each individual to awaken and surrender to it's presence, beginning at the point of surrendering to a higher power, while making the "call for help." This call will require one to be consistent and persistent in their seeking.

In a simplified way, the soul is at the center of the conscious self and the Monad is at the center of the soul. Master Jesus referred to the Monad as the Father when he said, "The Father and I are one." The soul is the intermediary between the conscious self (matter) and the Monad (spirit).

According to Trigueirinho, a Brazilian Spiritual Teacher, the soul holds the mental, emotional and physical-etheric permanent atoms in it's aura. Because of this interaction with the dense levels of existence (mental, emotional and physical-etheric), the soul's task of linking matter and spirit is limited until matter recognizes and surrenders to the omnipotence of the spirit. Through the permanent atoms the soul is able to introduce subtle impulses into external life.

When we make the conscious connection with our soul's light/love, we are able to decipher the impulses from the soul—the living code, and receive clear guidance in our daily life; bringing heaven to earth. Life becomes filled with power and grace, moving us from the mundane to the magnificent. In his book, *The Mystery of the Cross in the Present Planetary Transition*,

Trigueirinho says that when the potential of the soul is activated, "The soul becomes able to crucify the ego and to free itself from the play of forces of destruction and chaos [which] engulf most human beings."

Spirit: *Merriam-Webster's Collegiate® Dictionary* calls it the life principle, derived from the Latin word spiritus, meaning breath or to breathe. Dr. Carol Parrish-Harra in her book, *The New Dictionary of Spiritual Thought,* adds to this. She defines Spirit as the "...divine spark within each soul, the breath, or Spirit of God, i.e., Holy Spirit." Ancient scriptures say that God breathed into man the breath or spirit of life and he became a living soul. In this writing, we will use the words Holy Spirit and Divine Spirit interchangeably, with this definition in mind.

Spiritual: *Merriam-Webster's Collegiate® Dictionary* defines spiritual as being of the spirit; not corporeal. *The New Dictionary of Spiritual Thought,* states that it deals with the evolving soul following its own "...prompting and personal teachings of the spirit within self."

Spiritual Discontent: The driving force within that feels agitated and confused about a certain aspect of one's life, often prompting one to go beyond all logical reasoning of the mind and to question the sanity of one's belief system in search for answers. This is the aftermath of a "crossroads" event in life. There is a feeling of restlessness, prompted by a very intense desire to understand, "What on earth is going on in my life?" What can one do when life seems to hold no logical answer for what is transpiring in life, or the world as a whole? At this point the mind ambitiously seeks the guidance of a higher source and initiates the awakening of the soul, thus moving into the intuitive realm for spiritual guidance.

Spiritual Emergency: As implied, an emergency of the spirit. Just as a sudden injury to the physical body, is a physical emergency, it is the same with a spiritual emergency. A sudden shock to the spiritual body, by way of the belief system, can induce such an emergency. A physical emergency needs prompt care with a trip to the E.R., but where does one go for an emergency of the spirit? Where is the Spiritual E.R.?

In their book, *Spiritual Emergency*, Christina and Stanislav Grof explain that a spiritual emergency can leave us feeling lost in a void of our own feelings, our sense of self, and our place in the world as we know it.

Many asylums and sanitariums house souls that are going through a spiritual emergency. Their experiences can shake even the strongest person because they have no reference or safe point left in their shattered belief system. For some, like Eckhart Tolle author of *The Power of Now*, a spiritual emergency is experienced overnight and the person awakens to a totally new way of perceiving the world—a new state of consciousness; whereas, others (like us), thankfully, are experiencing a slower melt down.

Spiritual Experience: A very personal experience that goes beyond what is known as *normal*. A buzz word for it would be paranormal. This type of experience does not fit into the context of a traditional belief system— the letter-of-the-law religion. If you do not understand what is happening to you, it can often be frightening and puzzling. It is a personal experience with *something* but you are not sure *what*. This is often the catalyst for a spiritual journey that opens you to new concepts, and then you become like a *cosmic jumper cable*—connecting heaven and earth.

The Watcher: An aspect of our inner self, the soul, that begins to awaken when we consciously commit to making positive changes in our life. As we seek help to make these changes, the Watcher, our inner helper, reveals itself to us. We use the term "Watcher" interchangeably with the soul or higher self. It is a natural stabilizer to our emotional well being.

In the Bible story of the wise and foolish virgins, the Watcher would be the wise virgin who was always alert, conscious to what is happening in the surroundings, watching for intuitive messages, and observing thoughts, feelings, and emotions. You will know when you are in *"the Watcher mode,"* because you will feel as if you are both a detached observer and a participant in a current situation or aspect of your life—usually problematic. Our Watcher observes our life situations without judgments.

"To understand correctly what is taking place in your life, let go of purely human tendencies." "Listen to your most high consciousness and you will be safe." "Seek inner confirmation in your heart about all your decisions."
— *Calling Humanity* by Trigueirinho

"Everything occurs within the silence of the being. The more giving and empty the self becomes, the more it is exalted and unites with its own essence. *There is a moment in life when a certain key is turned, unlocking the entry to inner worlds.* And even though the entry should close again, the consciousness that glimpsed those inner worlds can no longer deny the existence of what it saw. Sooner or later there will be an advance in that direction."

— *Niskalkat* by Trigueirinho

Chapter 1

SPIRITUAL DISCONTENT

Coming Out of the Fog—
The Key to the Process of Spiritual Awakening

L ♫ Behind ALL the problems in the world, you will find the underlying currents of a discontented spirit. Within that discontent, you will find emotional currents with *fear* as the motivating factor. It is *fear* that also fuels these currents, keeping them alive and flowing.

In his book, *Stillness Speaks*, Eckhart Tolle states that the human consciousness must be transformed or humanity will destroy itself. A paradox presents itself as we observe our world getting better and worse at the same time. Negativity seems to dominate the world scene but Tolle says we are just more aware of the negativity because of the "noise" it is making.

Two emotions exist on the planet: love and fear. Each moment of our life is a choice between these two polarities. A split-second choice is made in the present moment from a subconscious level, based on our past experiences, and has a rippling effect through the rest of our life. When the choices come from fear, the consequences hold us captive in unhappy events—*our story.* We are clueless as to, *"Why is this happening to me again?"* or, *"How did I get into this situation?"*

These choices are in our face, daily, giving us ample opportunity to choose differently: love-forgiveness or fear-anger. On our evolutionary path today, our old choices are bowing before the new. We can no longer wallow comfortably in the aspects of our fear-based personalities; to do so will keep us on the path of self-destruction.

You are not traveling alone in this adventure. Your friend or foe is often right in your face, giving ample opportunity for *new choices of forgiveness*; teaching love, compassion, and tolerance. Our only option in these changing times is to get with the new program. This entails learning how to love not only our neighbor and *ourself*, but—equally important—learn to be at peace with our enemy and our life situation. Activation of *The Living Code* (TLC) in your life is one way to connect with the new program/paradigm, which will help you to perceive life in a new way.

The public display of rage in today's world is a reflection of an even greater inner rage. This inner rage reflects a *spirit of discontent* that is permeating the planet. Like a volcanic eruption, what you see on the surface is only a small part of the action. Today, volcanic anger is erupting in the most unlikely places, prompting us to ponder, *what on Earth is going on?*

The cosmic clock is ticking and we are finding our world at a crossroads, which explains why chaos seems to be the order of the day. Many seem to be confused, frozen in fear, as to the direction to take. It is imperative that we learn to connect to our intuition, to understand our direction in life.

We can no longer escape the consequences of our actions: personal, cultural, or global. We will reap what we have sown, *it IS the law!*

This spirit of discontent has been buried under layers and layers of emotional self-depression. When enough pressure builds up, a volcanic situation erupts in the world and/or in our personal life, thus beginning the shattering of these layers.

Like it or not, our karmic debt is surfacing. We are in the *days of truth*, and our negative/positive karma is surfacing to be balanced in order for us to move on to the next evolutionary step. Anything lacking integrity has got to go; nothing can be swept under the rug anymore. It MUST be dealt with in the present moment or suffer the boomerang effect of the karmic consequences—the cosmic two-by-four. Once we connect with the living code, our soul's purpose is to guide us through the maze of our karmic debt and get us back on the spiritual path.

As our new consciousness begins to surface, Spiritual Discontent arises, prompting us to seek a new level of spirituality. This is being shown in statistical information, revealing that people are looking for a different kind of spiritual nourishment—different from their parents and grandparents. Thus today, more and more people are saying that they are spiritual but not religious. For us, this means living by certain moral principles but following no particular religious doctrine. Also, like us, many have experienced life-transforming events, often prompted by spiritual discontent that shifts their perception of their current reality. Without meaning for it to happen, they eventually found themselves, like us, outside the box of organized religion.

On a deep personal level, when we decide to take responsibility for our choices and resulting actions, something wonderful begins to happen. It is as if an invisible hand begins to guide our life. As a result, life events begin to change and we begin to heal our wounded spirit, often having spiritual experiences as a part of the journey. We call this guidance our *Intuitive Guidance System* that follows a synchronistic flow that we call *The Living Code*. This "living code" is an underlying current residing in all of us, but only decipherable to those who know how to break the code.

This spiritual flow of *TLC* brings to our awareness spiritual experiences in coincidences—synchronistic events. More and more people have had at least one spiritual experience, a paranormal event in their lifetime. It comes in many forms, such as seeing angels, near death experiences, out-of-the-body experiences, hearing your name called inwardly, and many others. Faced with the risk of being ridiculed and condemned, you do not readily share these experiences and, no matter how hard others try to discount your inner experience, they cannot. Not being able to share inner experiences often leaves you feeling alone; relax, this is a normal response and part of the journey. Trust the process, and when the time is right, you will know when and with whom to share.

The Twins Reconnect

L & B ♫ Although we were identical twins, we each had our own spiritual agenda. Brenda's rebellious nature against the status quo of our religious upbringing, pulled her in one direction after high school, and Linda was pulled in the opposite direction and married a preacher. Although we received the same childhood upbringing, we share stories of how our life events affected each of us differently as we traveled similar karmic journeys.

As we went our separate ways after high school, our paradoxical twin journey began. This journey had many similarities to the Christian Bible story of the prodigal son's "home coming," where one son chose a "worldly" life and the other obedient son stayed home. As the prodigal child, Brenda headed out into the world to find her answers from life. Linda stayed home to seek answers within the boundary of traditional religion—following what she had been taught as "the gospel truth."

Disillusioned by the experiences in the world and the family religion, destiny reunited us. The "saint" and the "sinner," after a decade of experiences and very little communication, reconnected, realizing that we now had a 360° view of the prodigal son story. With a joined effort and a passion to seek truth, we pushed beyond the veil of illusion/deception of the world as we knew it— bringing heaven to earth by learning to decode life's hidden messages.

As this connection to our intuitive nature—a heart connection—began to solidify in our conscious awareness, it began to guide us through the mountain of karmic debt that was demanding payment.

We will relate, in this book, some of our personal experiences with spiritual discontent, spiritual experiences, and spiritual emergencies taken from our classroom of life. Not until we reconnected in our early thirties, did we have anyone with whom to share these experiences. At that time we connected on a new level—the spiritual level.

As you read these stories of our experiences, you may come to view your life in a different way and develop your own "living code." Our intention in this writing is to give you some ideas on how to start developing your own personal style of communication with Spirit, or to strengthen the connection you already have.

Divine Spirit used our life experiences as our teacher. These lessons taught us to come from a place of understanding that brought compassion rather than judgment. *Understanding* brings freedom from fear of the future, from guilt of the past, and forgiveness in the NOW. This freedom comes with a price called *responsibility*. We began to have a greater *ability to respond* in a non-reactive way to life's challenges when coming from a non-judgmental viewpoint. An inner peace began to reside within us as we observed the chaos in our lives. You will come to a deeper understanding, as we did, of the Bible verse, *"Do not judge, or you too will be judged."*

With this understanding, each moment brings with it the potential of a conscious or non-conscious choice. Will you choose to move beyond the free will dictates of the karmic-bound ego or choose the road less traveled of following the living code, dictated by the wisdom of your true intuitive nature—IGS?

Once you begin to move beyond the free will of the ego, you can then be guided by the light of the soul which renders you more conscious with each choice you make. This is the beginning of the journey to break the chain that binds you to your karmic debt. We will discuss more about this wonderful freedom in a later chapter.

Our Internal Background Music

Life is a song, a rhythm, playing background music all the time. There are many different stations—states of consciousness—on the dial. This music comes from our subconscious mind and overshadows every life event—from hard rock to easy listening! Most of us live and die still listening to the same station. Being twins seemed to turn up the volume, making us blatantly aware of what station we were habitually playing.

Each crossroad-moment, throughout life, brought us more under-standing about the music that constantly played in the background, our subconscious mind. At first, we did not realize that we had any power to change the station, let alone the type of music.

Slowly, we began to learn about the subconscious mind and the other stations that existed, besides the one we had been playing since childhood. We learned how to eliminate the emotional/spiritual pain that permeated our lives as a result of listening to just one station all the time. We learned that the music in our subconscious mind was activated by an unconscious symbolic guidance system.

Later in the book we discuss this symbology and how to replace it with a conscious Intuitive Guidance System. The IGS is a part of our spiritual matrix that helps bring harmony to our chaotic life. Once you begin to recognize the background music and the symbols attached to this music, you can begin to free yourself from life events that keep you locked in pain and suffering.

When the background music was triggered by one of our symbols and began to play, we learned that what we heard in the background affected the interpretation of everything we saw and experienced at that moment.

It is now known through quantum physics that we do not see with our eyes but with our mind. This is explained extremely well in the ground-breaking movie, *What the Bleep Do We Know!?* This movie explains what happens when we are looking for something and can't see it.

When we hold the thought/belief that something is not there, we actually can't see it and this confirms our belief, thus creating our reality. Upon asking someone to help, they easily find it "right under our nose"—bringing it into our awareness. This simple example helps us understand that another reality/dimension does exist and the experience helps us understand that we actually do not see with our eyes. We will share our experiences about this later.

Ponderism: *Could it be that we can't escape our painful background music until we become aware that it is holding us captive?*

If we had been born in a prison, (our cultural, religious, or mental/emotional conditioning) we would have no awareness of the need to escape. Our karmic background music is the bars that hold us captive and determines the color of the lens through which we view personal and world events.

How our childhood events are perceived and reinforced holds the bars in place and determines the hue of our lens. Later in the book, we mention other things that can, unknowingly, hold us captive. Because of their own personal subconscious-tinted lenses, three people who have watched an accident will perceive it three different ways. Why do you think it is wise to seek, at the very least, a second opinion?

As twins experiencing the same life events, we found the captivity phenomena very clear as we began to share our childhood stories. We often said, "I don't remember it happening just that way." or "I didn't feel that way about it."

How could this be possible when we had the same upbringing and witnessed the same events? Even though we were identical twins and born only minutes apart, it was obvious that our karmic background music was different, thus, dictating differing views of life's experiences.

It has been a lot of fun to compare the same life events and to understand how they impacted each of us differently. The parallels in our lives as twins are uncanny, often leaving us with a good laugh.

In a conversation one day as we were sharing what was happening in our lives, we humorously discovered that we were both buying new toilets.

How is it that both of us, without the other knowing it, decided—in the same week—to buy new toilets? How many times in a lifetime do you buy a new toilet? It makes one wonder if certain events are predestined—even the mundane ones.

Coming Out of the "Fog"—the Process of Spiritual Awakening

At this point, we feel it necessary to explain that our personal experiences are our perspective of *our story*—being told to help clarify a point. As you read this, perhaps you can better relate to, and understand, your personal experiences of spiritual discontent.

We refer to our karmic, unconscious background music as *the fog*. This fog is any obstacle that keeps us from knowing our True Divine Nature.

The Relationship Fog

Relationships seemed to be our most dysfunctional aspect. Eventually, life taught us that everyone in our relationships (father, mother, sibling, children, partner, etc.) was there for a special reason. We have come to refer to the difficult ones as *special relationships*. These special relationships played a valuable role in reflecting to us what we most needed to learn from life.

The relationships became a barometer which indicated what lesson we were working on, and our progress. Eventually, we became more interested in our progress than in taking the experience personally—don't take it personally! We bless, honor, and appreciate those people who played their part as our master teachers.

We share "our story" hoping that the reader will use it as a tool to grow spiritually from their own challenging life experiences. Once we learned to look at life from the "bigger picture," we saw the blessings in all of our experiences. At one point in Linda's journey, she leaned heavily on the Biblical verse stating that *all things work together for the good of those that love God*. At times, she really had to work hard at finding the good in a bad situation, but it was always there, just below the surface.

Eckhart Tolle in his book *Practicing the Power of Now,* brings more understanding to the spiritual dynamics that happens in our problematic relationships. Tolle explains that if you acknowledge that a problematic relationship is for your spiritual growth instead of the traditional way of thinking that relationships are here to *make you happy,* then that acceptance will set you free and, as we have observed, the relationship will change in some way.

The Generational Fog

Our mother and family were well intentioned in truly believing that they were responsible for saving our souls. We recall our Mother saying that she believed if all of her children didn't abide by our church doctrine—God's rules—she would go to hell. This explained so many of her actions in wanting to control our lives. From this example, we developed the understanding that love was conditional.

Our Mother was also raised without affection, as were many people of her generation. She held the common belief of her day that it was a woman's duty to give up her needs for the needs of others, especially her family, with no time to call her own. In our generation we have come to see this lack of self nurturing, which can develop into resentment and anger, creating many health challenges for women today.

> **Ponderism:** *How do I feel in my heart when I am being of service to my family and others?*

In the book, *Heal Your Body* by Louise Hay, she writes about the mental causes for physical illness. We have both used this small book for years in helping us to understand the mind-body connection. Her book explains that breast problems are, *"A refusal to nourish the self; Putting everyone else first; Over mothering; Overprotection; Overbearing attitudes."*

We have come to realize that instead of affection, our Mother showed her love by cooking wonderful food, sewing our clothes, and working in both the house and the fields. Her life on the farm with nine children was a never-ending job and life on the farm truly was not easy.

The Family Fog

Brenda refers to our early years as "the family fog." Our subconscious belief system—our background music—was founded in other peoples' perception of truth. This left us confused and unable to think or make decisions for ourselves. As a result, we grew up with the impression that someone outside of us had our answers, especially authority figures. Eventually, we began to ponder a major life question, "Is this the whole truth about life and God?" About the age of forty, after searching for answers for over a decade, the depressive "fog" began to lift.

In his book, *The Biology of Belief,* Dr. Bruce Lipton explains how your beliefs shape your health and your destiny, and that you are not controlled by your genes, you are controlled by your beliefs.

Ponderism: *If you could put aside, for a brief moment, all that you have been taught from childhood by parents, teachers, clergy, and anyone else, could you claim any original thoughts?*

Our parents grew up in what was called "The Great Depression" with a common religious belief; "spare the rod and spoil the child." Since vanity was not a virtue and compliments were given sparingly, our lives seemed to revolve around criticism, which, for us, created low self-esteem. Collectively, the end result seemed to produce a generation (the Baby Boomers) who, in the 1960's and '70's, were searching for their value in the form of what appeared to be rebellious actions against the status quo.

We have come to appreciate the fact that, had it not been for our strict religious upbringing, we might have chosen a more rebellious path with drugs or alcohol. Perhaps the bright side of this was a generation of seekers who dared to go beyond the status quo in the quest to find themselves.

It was not uncommon, as our generation grew up, to hear partners in marriage say, "I need to go find myself." When her husband left, Linda found herself caught in this situation, the "generational fog" of the early 1980's, at the birthing of what became known as "single parenting." We were not yet aware of being in a "generational fog" but knew that we did not have clarity about who we were. More often than not, in *the fog* we pointed the finger of blame toward others.

Major Crossroads in Life

What follows is a brief summary of life experiences that brought us to major life intersections—*the crossroads in life*. The leap of faith we took at these mile markers shifted our lives so dramatically that we now hardly recognize our former selves—leaving the past with dream-like qualities.

Our lives shifted dramatically when we experienced two crossroad moments at the age of nine. Our father died of a heart attack, and six months later, our house burned to the ground, taking all our possessions.

This truly left a void in our lives, teaching us how quickly life can rearrange itself, taking our sense of security with it. The fear and hardship our mother went through at this time must have been tremendous. She had relied on our father for almost everything, and now she was totally responsible for four children left at home.

After our house burned, we moved to a small town and gave up life on the farm. Having close neighbors was a new experience. When discussing the following story, we realized our thoughts were similar regarding Mother's comments about our neighbors' spiritual welfare.

After living in the small town for about a year and getting to know our neighbors, one day we gathered our courage to ask our Mother about the wonderful retired couple in our neighborhood. They had no children, and thus, adopted the neighborhood kids. We wanted to know if they were going to heaven. In our hearts, we both felt the ping of spiritual discontent as she replied to our spiritual question. Without hesitation she firmly replied, "No, they won't because they don't belong to our church."

For many years, we never thought to challenge this belief, and it deepened our fear of a punishing God. Not until this writing did we share how this event impacted our lives.

Brenda felt that if these wonderful people were going to burn in hell along with murderers and thieves, what chance did she have of living up to God's expectations? Linda felt confused and guilty. What if she had been born to this wonderful couple? With all the people in the world, how was it that she just happened to be born into the right family that had the only true religion? Her reply did not seem fair to our childish sense of equality.

We did not understand why people in other parts of the world, who had no chance of hearing our version of the truth, would be sent to hell. We knew better than to continue questioning our mother, and thus, held our spiritual discontent inside.

Linda's First Recollection of Spiritual Discontent

It was mid-afternoon as I stood on the playground of the old one-room school house. First grade seemed foreign to me as a right-brained, white-headed, freckle-faced child, and the fears I had collected in my six years of life began to make themselves known in a dyslexic way.

During mid-afternoon recess, very clearly I remember discussing with a few classmates the topic of God and salvation—the best a six-year-old could. I was trying to explain to them that they needed to be in the one true church in order to avoid hell.

My classmates left the playground when the bell rang. I turned toward the burning Midwestern afternoon sun with a desire that burned even brighter within my heart— a desire that others find God so that they would not have to go to this awful place the Bible called hell. A great sense of responsibility lay on my heart to help others find the truth.

As an imaginative, sensitive child, the threat of hellfire and brimstone left me with this awful fear of displeasing God. This resulted in an overwhelming need to be close to God and adamant about wanting to do God's will. This created an unhealthy emotional co-dependency on God that, for decades, played as my subconscious background music, influencing all major life choices based on my fear of God.

That day on the playground, I began to ponder about how one person could make a difference. Every Sunday morning and evening we went to church to hear the preacher give the plan of salvation to our rural, small-town congregation. I decided I wanted to be a preacher because it had to be the closest one could possibly get to God—my insurance policy to avoid the fire and brimstone of hell. Since the preacher studied the Bible daily, I figured that he surely knew God's will.

Then a cloud came over my grandiose thought of what it would be like to stand in the pulpit and have the words of God flow from my lips so fluently, the "Gospel Truth" as we called it. The cloud grew even darker as I began to come back from my fantasy world with the realization that our church did not allow women to take an active part in the worship service—especially as a minister! My dream began to crumble.

This was my first remembrance of spiritual discontent that carried with it a strong feeling of rejection and not being good enough. Why couldn't a woman be a minister? Did God like boys more than girls—men more than women? Even the Old Testament Bible stories were predominately about God and his relationship with men; women always seemed to play a lesser role, often treated the same as servants or slaves.

Something I had no control over—my gender—stood in the way of my aspirations. These feelings of being inferior to men in God's eyes would reappear over and over in my life in many forms, setting up the proverbial battle of the sexes over equality.

My only problem was that I didn't like to compete, because someone had to lose. I have come to realize how emotionally empathic Brenda and I were in feeling others' emotional pain. Our two-room school house had burned and we had to attend a school some distance from our home. This came in the middle of the second grade and was emotionally hard for me.

When the teacher told the class of a misdeed and wanted to know who did it, I remember feeling guilty even though I was innocent. When I related this story to Brenda, she acknowledged feeling the same way. Unknowingly, Brenda and I were little psychic sponges-empathic; picking up bits and pieces of everyone's emotional garbage. This explained to me why I felt guilty. With this self-knowledge, I could begin to understand some of my emotional nature and determine if what I was feeling was really my emotion or someone else's.

As I grew older, I was asked the obvious childhood question, "What do you want to do when you grow up?" Since I could not be a minister, I did not know how to respond. Life decisions were based on this one attitude of "not good enough for God"—unworthiness was the real issue.

By the time I graduated from high school, I was convinced that the only way to get in God's good graces, avoid hell, and be guaranteed that my children not go to hell, was to marry a preacher. As this background music played, I decided the best option was to attend a Christian college and find a preacher. I was married one year later, assuming the identity of "the preacher's wife."

Brenda's Recollection of Spiritual Discontent

"God is too Big to Fit into One Religion!" This bumper sticker held a profound message for me, because it appeared when I began to write this segment about my personal journey with the family's religious beliefs, and its impact on my life—the journey from "sinner" to "saved," but not in the traditional way.

As Linda mentioned, I was a sensitive child and often took things too personally; yet, of the two of us, I was more of the rebel. I didn't want to conform so easily to the many rules that were not to be questioned, but which didn't make sense to my young "free spirited" mind.

I was very inquisitive, with too many questions that my mother didn't want to address or encourage. Even at a young age, my little "inquiring mind" wanted things to make sense before I fully embraced them. It would be many years before I fully understood that no matter how *normal* I appeared or tried to be on the outside in order to fit in, I truly walked to the beat of a different drummer. Today, I would be diagnosed as having DDD, the *Different Drummer Disorder*.

Also, the *Gullibility Disorder* was quite ingrained, even into my early twenties. I was so gullible that in the late 1980's I awoke one morning with a male voice inside my head emphatically saying, "Stop being so naïve." This was a startling moment and my first experience of this nature—it jolted me awake! I had an immediate knowing that this related to my relationship with my husband. In my naïveté, I truly thought that since lying was a sin, as the Bible said, that others also held this belief and, thus, would always be honest with me. This helped me understand why I was so quick to accept the family religious fog. They were merely in their *gospel truth* and knew it was their responsibility to save me from burning somewhere for all of eternity.

My first recollection, at age six, was much different than Linda's spiritual aspirations, yet very relevant to my spiritual growth. My spiritual discontent didn't begin with just one event; it was many subtle, and not-so-subtle, events along the way. These events would serve as a catalyst to light the fire within my spirit to search for truth beyond the family fog. It would be many years before I understood that getting to heaven was an inside job.

We studied the Bible "religiously" and learned from the Old Testament about an angry, punishing God. As a six-year-old, the fear of God was instilled even deeper in me one evening during a family dinner. I mentioned what I thought was a great new word that I had just heard at school. The word "golly" barely escaped my lips when, to my horror, my Mother came charging at me. In a fight-or-flight moment, my only recourse was flight.

Today, I find humor in the picture of her frantically chasing me around the dinner table. As usual, this ended with a spanking for my transgression which, until now, hadn't included the spoken word. The word "golly" was blasphemy; a "sin word" never to be used again. Where was I when God passed out the "sin word memo?" Unfortunately, the list was made over the years through trial, but mostly error, and included, but was not limited to: darn, hell, hate, damn, and gosh. This brought much confusion—heaven forbid if I had ever said any of the "real" four-letter words.

My mother's intention of saving her children from hell explained why, as we approached the dating age, it was made clear that we could only date boys of our faith—and the "pickin's were slim." The lack of affection in our family, combined with our father dying when we were young, caused me to be so starved for affection that I latched onto the first boy who showed the slightest interest.

I survived those years in the fog by detaching through the useful, but not often appreciated, art of daydreaming, resulting in recalling very little of my childhood experiences. Eventually, my familys' intolerance of my inquiring mind—wanting to know—broke my spirit. I stopped asking questions and went into a coma-like state, trying to fit into the "normal" slot as defined by my family and their religious perceptions.

About the age of twenty-five, the accumulated spiritual discontent caught up with me. My self-esteem was at an all-time low, I was in an unhappy marriage, depressed, confused, and alone with no one to turn to—not even God. Confiding in Linda wasn't an option at this time, as she was still in the family religious fog and married to a minister I didn't like. Divorce was out of the question because of my religious beliefs, and returning home was not an option.

For over seven years, I hadn't prayed to God for help because I was in the "sinner" category and, therefore, out of hearing-range of the Divine. I had stopped attending the family church, causing my Mother to say, "I never thought you would turn out like this." At this point in my "wandering in the wilderness of spiritual discontent," I wasn't even sure there was a God and if He was as mean and intolerant as I had been taught; I wasn't sure I even wanted Him in my life. I was raised by the letter-of-the-law doctrine and realized this system wasn't feeding my soul. The knowing came that no matter how much

I attended church, I still had spiritual discontent—it was like a hole inside my heart that wasn't being filled. Thus began many deep, heart-felt ponderings— "Was this all there was to life?" This deep discontent eventually led to "the call for help" which we will explore next.

"From the Holy Spirit's gentle, guiding hand,

I learned that paranormal experiences

were tools Spirit used to get my attention,

but were not the ultimate goal." — **B** ♫

"The supernatural is the natural not yet understood."
— Neale Donald Walsh

Chapter 2

THE CALL FOR HELP LEADS TO SPIRITUAL EXPERIENCES

My-Way, Your-Way, or the Higher-Way

*The Call is the key that unlocks
the doorway to the heart.*

---

*"Through surrender a far-reaching transformation silently
begins beneath what the eyes see and the senses perceive."*

— *Trigueirinho*

L ♫ Everyone who experiences chronic discontent, comes to a crossroad called *desperation*. At this crossroad we all have the same realization, "I can't handle my life as it is." In excruciating emotional pain, something deep within us puts forth "the call"—a cry for help.

An inner shift takes place and on bent knees, we say, "I don't know which way to go—show me the way!" Even those who don't believe in God put forth the call to "something" outside of themselves for help. "If there is a God, please HELP me!"

In spite of outer appearances, rest assured when making the call for help that NO CALL goes unheard!

This is a profound moment of authentic surrender. From this point on, there is no turning back as your life begins the very subtle transformation that something deep within you has initiated. Sounding forth this call, puts an inner invisible High-way beneath your feet—referred to in spiritual writings as *the journey home* or *the path*.

The action of surrendering is, in essence saying, "Not my will but Yours *be done.*" Letting go and letting God takes intense, quiet initiative on your part. The action of surrender, as discussed in the next chapter, turns into active listening to God. This active surrendering involves giving up, but not in the way you might think. What you are "giving up," or surrendering, is the *free will* of the ego, often referred to as the personality ego, little self, lower self, worldly man (Bible), etc. This aspect of the ego has led mankind to where it is today and the necessity to either change or face extinction.

The ego, as Eckhart Tolle says in *The Power of Now*, is a mental image of who we think we are, formed during childhood, and based on our personal and cultural conditioning. Tolle refers to the analytical mind, "the thinker," and the false created self as the ego. Any references to ego in this book will have this definition.

Tolle further explains in, *Practicing the Power of Now*, that our freedom begins when we realize that we are not "the thinker." A higher level of consciousness is activated the moment we start becoming the Watcher of our thought (the ego). In doing this you become aware of a vast realm of intelligence beyond thought. He also relates that everything that truly matters comes from beyond the mind—joy, inner peace, love and creativity.

Ponderism: *Could our ego-mind be a contributing factor to our problematic life situations?*

The Journey of Soul Begins

"*I am open to the education that is inspired by my Soul.*"
— *The Angel of Education*

Once the call is made, and surrendering the desires (free will) of the ego puts our life events in the hands of something greater within ourselves—the soul. I like to think of it as tuning to a higher frequency. Then, we are consciously choosing to change the genetic and cultural background music that we have listened to for many lifetimes. For most of us, the journey is made in increments; having completed the lesson given, we move on to the next lesson or step, then the next. There is always one more step on the path.

While writing this, I was nudged to pull an *Angel Meditation* card for the day and, surprisingly, it fit right into this segment—duh!

"True knowledge comes to us when we tune in to the Soul. All that we receive from the external world is second-hand information. Direct knowledge is something we can contact when we realize it is already within ourselves. Education is allowing the Soul's latent wisdom to manifest itself, teaching us how to live."

In the past, only a small number of people were in contact with the soul level. Humanity now has an opportunity to tap into this intuitive aspect of the soul and awaken the powerful, sleeping giant within. Many refer to this as the Divine Feminine energy, which is the inevitable evolutionary stage that humanity is now entering.

As we acknowledge and accept into our life the impulses of the soul, our life events begin to re-arrange themselves in a synchronistic way—as if guided by an invisible force, which is almost palpable at times. The obstacles created by the free will choices of the ego, which keep God's love at bay, will begin to crumble. Our chaotic life events may actually increase as soul organizes and rearranges our karma; making our life events into instruments of testing, learning, and spiritual growth.

This is the shortest path home—going through the mountain of chaos with the soul forging the way. Your job of staying out of the ego's clutches and staying awake, while following the path, greatly enhances your ability to tune into the frequency of this Intuitive Guidance System.

The Problem Created by Free Will

Ponderism: *Is free will really FREEING?*

We are often quite proud of individualistic choices made by our free will. Yet, when I read in the book *Beyond Karma* by Trigueirinho that free will is what the ego uses to make choices, I had to ponder it for a while to grasp the full concept of its meaning.

"The gift of free will, the principle, is one of the instruments by which the ego learns and is strengthened. But at more advanced stages of the evolutionary path, free will begins to hamper the soul's progress."

You can't solve a problem with the same mind that created it. You have to tune into the frequency of the "Higher-way" in order to get a different perspective of the problem before it can be solved. Then, apply the insight gained to the problem and see what happens.

This is the *Heaven to Earth* problem-solving question, *"How can I perceive this in a different way?"* When I have a problem I can't resolve, I simply say, *"I don't know the solution to this situation. I surrender it to God/ Higher Will—not my will, but Your Will be done."*

Be persistent in surrendering the solution; the ego will eventually give up and stop thinking of solutions to the problem. Every time I surrender the free will of the ego and stop the mind from thinking about the problem, the situation seems to take care of itself. It's amazing how other people, with out knowing it, help you resolve your problems. If a problem is persistent, I wait, trusting the guidance of the soul and the fact that there is right timing for everything, especially solutions.

"It is said that all roads lead back home to God. The journey to God is merely the reawakening of the knowledge of where you are always, and what you are forever. It is a journey without distance to a goal that has never changed."
— A Course in Miracles

Willingness to Look at New Concepts
—Linda's Spiritual Discontent Leads to the Call

Often, people are not open to new ideas until they are almost on their death bed—literally or figuratively. It's like a last resort option, and the thought is, *"What have I got to lose, maybe I should try something different?"*

In the following story I will relate the "spiritual death bed" experience that prompted me to look at new concepts that were often contrary to my former beliefs. This story is about my fight for spiritual survival, even to the point of literally making a *pact with God*—totally unaware of the consequences of my decision.

As I mentioned in the last chapter, I attended a Christian college to become a preacher's wife. I envisioned the Cinderella story of getting married and living happily ever after, but I soon found that this naive perception was more like the *Cinderella Disorder.*

The first clue that something was not quite right with this relationship came on our honeymoon when he mentioned not wanting to hold my hand. This finally made sense to me in the last year of our troubled marriage. One day while I was pondering the situation, an inner voice spoke one unbelievable word: homosexual.

As I began to entertain this insight, I went into denial because of the obvious consequences and changes this truth could bring to a preacher's wife with two young children. Denial did not stop the inevitable from happening— the fourteen-year marriage ended in divorce. The truth finally came out of the closet; his agony became more and more painful and he wanted to be free—to find himself.

Later, I remember feeling compassion for him when he told me the real reason he left. How sad it was to think of all the times I had heard him preach against homosexuals and now to know he was condemning himself. I began to understand that his anger (vented at me) actually came from the inner rage he felt for himself. I concluded that his pain had to be greater than mine, and I told him I understood why he had to go. Inwardly I was relieved to be free of this roller coaster relationship ride.

I have since come to realize how much we identify with "who we think we are," and how important my identity was as the preacher's wife. Still feeling that God was partial to men, I had used this identity to get closer to God— now what? Life had just given me an "identity crisis." This one event proved to be my wake-up call and the catalyst for my spiritual awakening.

The design of what I thought God wanted me to do with my life came to a devastating end. Where did I go wrong? I could not blame God for my troubled life events, so I concluded the problem had to be me. Those Old and New Testament stories from childhood came back to haunt me on a subconscious level—God punishes sinners. Was I being punished for something—if so, what was it? I put forth *the call* for help, mixed with the attitude of—*why me, God?*

The Shift Happened—Linda's Version

Not too long after the divorce, a close church member gave me a different version of the Bible, the New International Version (NIV). Since I was feeling as if I were on the spiritual death bed, I was willing to try something different—even if it was not the authorized King James Version (KJV) of the

Bible that many people in our church used.

When I began reading the NIV, it was as if I had never read the Bible before. The clarity that it held for me was ecstatically refreshing and freeing. I could understand it so much better than the KJV. It soon became clear that something was shifting within me. When I read a passage, the little recorder inside my head that always played the KJV interpretation was noticeably quiet. It was fascinating how changing and rearranging a few words from the literal translation put a different slant on my old ideas—giving me powerful new insights to ponder.

I had always stayed within the church doctrine's interpretation of the Bible. I knew all too well the ramifications of crossing that boundary line. Not liking confrontations kept me silent about what I was studying, and so I pondered alone.

I became obsessed with reading every passage in the NIV Bible that related to the Holy Spirit. I never recalled anyone in our church mentioning guidance from the Holy Spirit, God, or even Jesus Christ.

Since there was no "witnessing for Christ" in our conservative church, I knew very little about the concept. All of this made me ponder how the Holy Spirit and miracles would guide me into "all truth" if I didn't believe it was active in my daily life. I was taught that the Holy Spirit existed in the first century merely to help get the church started. I pondered about how they thought God answered prayers, if not by the Comforter that Jesus said he would send. I had sat in Bible study classes all my life and had no recall of this topic being studied or discussed. Thus, I had many unanswered questions that I kept to myself.

Crossing the Boundary Line by Surrendering to the Holy Spirit

For me, confusion began to settle in as it usually does when new information collides with old belief systems. It is human nature to feel threatened and fearful when your spiritual beliefs come under question, even if the questioner is yourself. But thankfully, I didn't nail this version of the Bible to the cross. My Spiritual "headache" was now reaching migraine level, and I had reached a point of no return. This was a point of total surrender. It became very clear what I had to do in spite of what the church had taught me. *I needed to ask the Holy Spirit to be the guiding force in my life!*

Unknown to me then, this was a surrender of what I now call my free will. This began the far-reaching, subtle transformation beneath what the eyes could see and the ears could hear. I now know I was surrendering the free will of the ego as I stepped into a whole new world of a Spirit-led life—*not my will but thy will be done*—became my motto.

I pondered how I might open a line of communication with the Holy Spirit that I now believed was possible. Questions entered my mind. How would I know when the communication lines were open? The following story reveals my plan.

Making a Pact with God

An idea came to me from some of the Old Testament stories I knew, where God was asked to give two signs as an indication for truth in the direction to be taken. I also recalled that two witnesses were required for truth in a trial. Even some of the key people in the Old Testament asked God for two confirmations of His will for them, and it was given.

I finally had a plan; I would ask the Holy Spirit to send the message to me twice. To make sure that the message was from the Holy Spirit and that I had heard correctly, I asked that the two messages come from totally different sources—same answer, but two sources. Amazingly, it began to work!

Becoming the Watcher

By this time, my mind was full of questions as to the direction my life should take. Over time, I became a very keen Watcher or observer of my life events as every moment could hold a message. As my focus changed, my depression began to lift. Instead of being depressed about my life situations, I felt a new, inner excitement—hope.

The communication system I had set up with Holy Spirit was working and, as my faith grew, so did my bond with It. With my Intuitive Guidance System riding shotgun, I walked forward through my mountain of karmic debt no longer in intense fear of what lay ahead. I had learned how to bring the *Higher-Way* to Earth, and as I learned to balance each situation, my life experiences became the lessons in the textbook.

I often find it humorous, wondering how many times the messages were sent in those early days while I was learning to become the Watcher, until

I could stay in the present moment long enough to recognize them.

I didn't always like the answers I received, but I had to honor my pact with God and, as a result, I came to trust the Source completely. I came to enjoy the excitement of the new journey that my questions to God prompted. Life became alive with information—*The Living Code*—as I learned to follow the dictates of Spirit and found myself feeling like Dorothy in the Wizard of Oz trying to get home on the yellow brick road.

The Call Leads to Spiritual Experiences

A transition point came about six months after my divorce. My two children and I lived in a very modest small house. Early one morning, while I was in the twilight zone of half-asleep, half-awake—I heard the voice. Very clearly, a soft, unearthly male voice called my name—"Linda!" I was startled, but not frightened. The voice came from the direction of my closed door. I lay there thinking of how, in the Bible, Samuel heard God calling his name.

Puzzled as to what this meant, I did not share this with anyone for a long time. Those in my religion would deny my experience, giving the credit to the Devil, just as my mother had said that dreams were of the Devil.

I had learned early on to be discerning about whom I shared my spiritual experiences with. I knew that being different invokes fear in many people, especially when it involves religion or something they don't understand. Historically, many women have been burned at the stake because they spoke of their intuitively-guided experiences, and I was not yet ready for that experience. Metaphorically, that would come a few years later when, because of my energy healing work (Touch for Health Kinesiology), some of the family literally thought Brenda and I were witches.

Brenda's Spiritual Discontent Leads to the Call

B ♫ My desperate call for help began around the age of twenty-five, in the mid-1970's. Linda perfectly described it at the first of this chapter; I was in chronic discontent and at the crossroad called "desperation."

I had gotten married right out of high school, thinking the path to living happily ever after was marriage and giving my life over to my new husband. Linda and I both had the Cinderella Disorder. My self-worth and happiness were tied to other peoples' approval, so I became an exceptional "goody two-shoes—people pleaser." Initially, the self-sacrifice to please others seemed a small price to pay to have their approval, but eventually, it proved to be my undoing. The more I said yes to others, the further I grew from my Intuitive Guidance System.

After seven years of living in my "happiness plan," it all began to crumble, leaving me feeling alone, confused, and hopeless. We no longer attended the family church, which brought feelings of deep guilt because this put me in the category of a "sinner." And the family religion taught that God didn't hear the prayers of sinners, so I had stopped praying.

In my mind, this left me no one to turn to as Linda was still steeped in the family religion and, thus, unapproachable. Out of sheer desperation, I made the call (prayer) for help. With all my heart I prayed—if there is a Higher Power, please show me the way—I need a sign NOW! Would the real God please stand up?

This Call for help was the beginning of my conscious awakening from the spellbinding, programming of the teachings of my youth and the quest for answers to my question, "Is this all there was to life?" I felt a deep inner void in my heart, like a black hole looming closer—threatening to consume me.

The Shift Happened—Brenda's Version

Soon after my prayers for help, things began to happen in my life that would totally redefine my belief system. In my youth, we often read the Bible and adhered to the family's religious interpretation as the only "gospel truth." Not knowing where else to start, I turned back to the Bible for one more read. It felt like I was reading it for the first time; words leapt off the pages with a newness of life, hope, and inspiration. How could I have missed this understanding all these years?

This new understanding shook the very core of my spiritual foundation, as if everything I had been taught was now turned upside down. Unknowingly, I had begun my lifelong quest for spiritual truth and the fire of Spirit had been lit; there was no turning back.

My desperate call for help was a profound point of surrender, creating the necessary shift to the Holy Spirit's helping hand. Unknowingly, I had moved out of the rigid mental interpretation of the Bible—the letter-of-the-law perception—into a more compassionate place from my heart—the spirit of the law perception.

I also realized that I didn't really know how to pray. The only prayers I had heard were in church or at the dinner table, and they seldom changed. To me, they sounded more mechanical than from the heart. Again, I turned to the Bible for help. It suggested that to become a Spirit-led person, my new goal, my prayer should be to ask the *Spirit of Truth (Holy Spirit)* to guide my heart. It also said to ask that you be guided in spirit and in truth, in wisdom and knowledge, and ask for inner peace and understanding. This became a lifelong prayer.

Brenda's Call Leads to Spiritual Experiences

B ♪ My call for help was answered with many experiences that were outside the box of normal life experiences; a wake-up call from Spirit that was very necessary to my spiritual growth. The Master Jesus said that unless we are born again, of the Spirit—not the flesh—we could not enter the kingdom of God. This awakening of my Inner Spiritual Self was like a re-birthing. My perception of life, Spirit, and the Universe changed dramatically. As the old beliefs were cleansed by the fire of Spirit, a new self emerged from the ashes— the Spirit-led life began. There would be many more crossroads to face, but this time I had a new invisible Helper.

This was a lonely path as these "outside-the-box" experiences were some that my family and religion could neither explain nor wanted to address. Anything outside their teachings was from the Devil—there was no debating this. I pondered how this inner-loving presence could be from the Devil.

My dreams became dramatically vivid, and some felt more real and alive than my waking life. The Bible said to, "try the spirits" and "faith without works is dead," so I, very discerningly, ventured forward, testing all that was given to me. This was, unknowingly, developing an inner faith from personal experience that no one could take from me. I was no longer at the mercy of others' perceptions, nor man-created rules. Nothing in my traditional Christian upbringing prepared me for the experiences that followed.

In the mid-1970's, my quest for truth brought several synchronistic events. One of them happened when a temporary co-worker gave me a small book; reading it was a life-altering experience—*There Is A River*, by Edgar Cayce. The information in this one small book served to be the most freeing of anything I had read, outside of the Bible.

Edgar Cayce was a devoutly religious man who had paranormal experiences that shook the core of his belief system, and spiritual foundation to which I could relate. He had visions, visits from angels, and vivid dreams.

His work taught me the importance of dream interpretation and meditation, and it opened me to the concept of life after death—reincarnation. This fueled the fire within, prompting my inquiring mind to search for more.

The Edgar Cayce material led me to Elsie Sechrist's book, *Dreams: Your Magic Mirror: With Interpretations of Edgar Cayce.* This began my lifelong study and journaling of dreams. I was beginning the path of self-understanding which would eventually redefine my belief system.

The first "foundation-shaking" dream started in a large shopping mall—only a woman would have a spiritual dream in a shopping mall! What startled me most was the crystal clear, male voice that spoke inside my head: "There is more truth than what is in your Bible." I had been taught, and believed, that the King James Bible held the only "gospel truth." I knew that the act of shopping was a symbol indicating a search for something of value; in my case it was *truth.* The many shops indicated there was more than one option as I had been shopping only in the King James Bible store...our church's authorized edition.

As the dream suggested, I reluctantly began to search for, and read, many other religious writings—actually, with the initial intention to prove them wrong. Finally, after much scrutiny, I had to humbly admit that other Spiritual Masters had walked the earth and had similar life stories, including a virgin birth and a traumatic death. Their messages held a common theme about love, forgiveness, and compassion; the very teachings of Christ.

In the late 1970's I had my first vision. I had been taught that visions only happened to people in the Bible. During a mundane chore one morning I clearly saw, in my mind's eye, an open book. The pages held an adaptation of two familiar Bible verses: *"Seek ye first the kingdom of God and his righteousness and all these things will be added unto you,"* and a second verse, *"Love the Lord your God with all your heart and soul and your neighbor as yourself."* Unknowingly, these simple verses held the key to "my salvation" and would be ones that I would ponder for most of my life.

The 1980's held many foundation-shaking moments. The following is a very brief summary of some of the more significant ones.

My first angel visit came as I awakened one night to find a very real person, a man, sitting at the foot of my bed. As our eyes met, I was flooded with an overwhelming feeling of unconditional love—a feeling I had never felt in my entire life. This spiritual experience left me with the understanding that I would be okay. The timing was perfect as I had some deep questions and felt very insecure about my marriage. This encounter dissolved many of my fears and gave me the hope that kept me going.

In 1986, I was led to a couple of books and, in conjunction with meditation, I started having out-of-body experiences. Initially, I was scared as my spirit lifted out of my body toward the ceiling. But soon I learned to relax, resulting in an incredible feeling of aliveness and freedom.

These experiences released my fear of death as I walked through the veils of time into the past and future, and other dimensions, where life was much different than on earth. The fabric of these unknown worlds felt more real than my daily life—I pondered, how could this be? I also thought of the Bible, in the book of Revelations written by St. John, when he mentioned the different heavens. Is this what was happening to him when he spoke of being "in the Spirit?"

Over the years, paranormal experiences fueled my quest for truth in the search for my true identity. Sometimes I would awaken in the night hearing my name called, a phone ringing, or occasionally a loud explosive sound in my head—could this be spiritual dynamite for those tough, habitual patterns.

The seemingly miraculous experiences brought truths that stretched my limited perspectives about life, God, and the Universe. With each experience, I would always be discerning, studying, and questioning—a hound of heaven. At the time there were few books explaining what was happening to me. Today, I realize that the gentle hand of the Holy Spirit was leading me down the lonely path of self-realization. In the end, I learned that *paranormal experiences were tools Spirit used to get my attention, but were not the ultimate goal.*

In the following chapters we will explore our communication signals with the Divine Spirit.

Chapter 3

GOD IS TALKING—ARE YOU LISTENING?

Learning to Decipher the Hidden Messages

Many millennia ago, God called together all the wise ones in heaven for their opinions on where they should hide the key to life for the humans. Many interesting ideas were submitted and considered by these holy beings. They finally agreed that God's proposal was the best of the lot: "Considering the nature of these beings, the last place they will look is within, so that is were we will place it. Then I will provide passion to torment them until they find it."

— source unknown

By Linda with B's ♫

Most of us have heard at some time in our life, the age old question: *If a tree falls in the forest, would it make a sound?* This question has been debated for eons. In the book, *The Disappearance of the Universe* by Gary Renard, this paradoxical question is addressed and explained. Thanks to Gary, I don't have to spend the rest of my life pondering this one!

His book explains that in order for something to make a sound it has to have a receiver, otherwise it is just another inaudible frequency traveling through space. Therefore, the answer is: without an ear to hear—a receiver— no sound is made.

This explanation gives us a clue about how to turn on the inner hearing aid that links us to this key to life. ALL humans are searching for this link—we have to be tuned-in and turned-on to the right frequencies. If we will but ask, God will lead us on the path to this key to life—the kingdom within. Like the parable in the Bible of the wise and foolish virgins, you have to stay alert; be in the present moment, anticipating God's signal.

When we have a seeking, heartfelt question, we are turning the dials on the cosmic radio, searching for a particular station that is broadcasting our answer. Our seeking transmits the signal and like a radio antenna, also receives the answers. Without this focused intention, we just get a lot of static that I call *humanity's karmic background music*—mental white noise. The more we focus on and practice listening to God's messages, the better we get.

A great hindrance to receiving our answers is the subconscious programming that many of us were taught as children from our Christian Bibles, *"It is more blessed to give than to receive."* So, on a subconscious level, we feel we are unworthy to receive God's answers or love.

Ponderism: *God is always talking, but are we really listening?*

We have always been a part of God/Source, but because of our programming, we are led to believe that we are sinners and not worthy of God's love. This simply is not true! We are the curtain that keeps the *Sun* (of God) from shining on us. It is up to us to drop the curtain (veil) that separates us from our eternal Source—Guidance. Each time we ignore our intuitive nudges, the curtain thickens, and the room grows darker. If we learn from those times when we failed to listen to the inner voice, then nothing has been lost. The more we become the Watcher, the thinner the veil becomes, and the light within grows brighter—we are the light of the world.

When I made a pact with God (mentioned in Chapter Two) I wanted, without a doubt, to make sure I knew when God was talking. That is why I asked for the messages to come my way twice, from different sources, but with the same specific message. When I wanted specific information about a topic, I had to put it on the back burner in my mind—making it a ponderism. Then it became a matter of learning to listen while observing what was happening in my life circumstances—the Watcher in me, as mentioned before, became stronger. I also found I could not talk and listen at the same time. I had to quiet my mind so that I could be alert, which kept me in the present moment.

My pact with God is a good example of making the call/sound (broadcasting) with enough force to be heard. I was going to "hound God" with my unanswered questions about why my life was "hell" until I got a reply—period! If what I had been reading in the Bible was true, then the Holy Spirit had to reply—it was a spiritual law; a*sk and receive—seek and find—knock and the door will open.*

In order for the Holy Spirit to reply, I had to become a receiver of the sound that the Holy Spirit made as referenced in the Bible: *"He who has ears let him hear."* We both had to be on the same wave-length in order to communicate. When I was sure of God's will for me I could walk with confidence, knowing, without a doubt, that I was headed in the right direction.

Tuning In To Divine Guidance

B ♫ Our childhood programming included nothing about how to listen to God or that we could even receive Divine Guidance. As I mentioned before, the angry punishing God was the only one I knew. I was taught to fear God and keep his commandments, and because of this I felt God was unapproachable. The only resources I had for the interpretation of the Bible were others' opinions—preachers and parents.

Of course this brought me to the crossroad of spiritual discontent and despair, as mentioned in the previous chapter. Unknowingly, this divine plan that created such inner and outer turmoil in my life experiences actually held the very key to activating my inner hearing aid and, thus, I learned to listen with my heart. This spiritual discontent created an inner resistance to "what is," which was the key to fuel a rocket of desire for something better, leading me to the call for help. My life was a roller coaster ride, until my forties, when I finally began to listen within more than without.

With my cosmic receivers "tuned-in and turned-on," my life experiences began to reflect this switch. Eventually, I realized that when I continually surrendered my power to anyone outside of myself, there were dire consequences in what was best for me—self sacrifice wasn't the key to happiness as I had thought and been taught. I still had many challenging experiences, but now I had help in making better choices. As I began to focus more on listening within, the gap or time delay between making the call for help and receiving the answer began to shorten.

People are Searching for Something!

L ♫ Testimonial to the fact that people are looking for something is the crowded bookstores and the abundance of knowledge sitting on the shelves. Somewhere, someone is searching for something, finding themselves in science, religion, politics, healing arts, and all other fields of human endeavor. Some can even sense, or are aware, that on a deeper level something is missing in life but they are not sure where to find it, often leaving them depressed for unknown reasons. Could it be the *call of the Soul*—the subtle messages replying to the inner longing for an understanding about life, wanting inner peace and seeking happiness?

When Religion Does Not Have Your Answers
—Whom DO You Listen To?

Brenda and I found ourselves, like so many others, in a situation where our former religious beliefs were clashing with what our inner guidance was telling us. We have come to be neither for nor against any one religious system. We have come to a place of understanding that each person is responsible for *working out their own salvation* (NIV Bible) in whatever form they may be guided.

Whether you call God by the name of Buddha, Allah, Great Spirit, Jehovah, Source, or any other name, makes no difference to us. Our focus is on finding the inner guidance, also called by many names—Holy Spirit, Higher Self, Inner Self, Guardian Angel, Ascended Master, guides, etc. Make up your own name—the Source is the same! The truth is we are all seeking our Inner Guidance System no matter what we call it.

B ♫ I have already related my journey out of organized religion and onto the spiritual path. I always like the analogy that came to me many years ago after hearing others say, including the religion of my youth, that their way, method, belief, is better or more powerful than the others—they had the "only way" and wanted you to follow them. As I pondered this concept later in life, I received a visual analogy as one way for me to view God. On my inner screen, I saw a large, beautiful, wise old tree which was an eternal, all-present energy connecting heaven and earth. Humanity is like the branches on the tree. So how could anyone declare that one branch (one way) is better than another, or has the only "gospel truth?"

If you want to believe that someone else's way is better for you, then you will have the experience of following another until you realize that you too can easily connect to the same Source. Thus it would make sense to listen within—to the heart's intuitive knowing.

Work Out Your Own Salvation

L ♫ The IGS will take you where ever you need to go to "work out your own salvation" once you plug into the system/frequency and become a receiver/listener. The IGS may indeed connect you with a certain religion, person, or book. Once you learn what you need from that connection, you may or may not move on. If you are following your IGS, it really won't matter where you are, because it will be the best place for you in any given moment. That makes life so much simpler—no fuss about needing to be in any one place or religion to communicate with God. Since Life is ever evolving, you will be in a flow that is never ending. Talk about perpetual motion—you are it!

God is Definitely Talking But Do I Dare Take the Step?

L ♫ I will share an experience of following my IGS based on my making a pact with God.

Four years had passed since I had set up this communication technique with Spirit. As my confidence grew, each test of faith seemed to stretch me a little further. My diligence in learning to receive Spirit's messages was beginning to pay off. Even though life was still chaotic, there was an element of excitement each time I realized that I was in the miracle moment of receiving communications from the Holy Spirit.

I had no choice but to take my life one step at a time and to not speculate about the future, which I knew from childhood experiences could/would change in a flash.

As mentioned previously, I was now reading a different version of the Bible than the traditional King James Version. I had studied all the scriptures referencing the Holy Spirit and began to search for other books written about the Spirit of God.

The opportunity came one day when I took my daughter to the library. While she was busy, I decided to browse the book-shelves, and I filtered through several book titles until one caught my attention: *The Winds of*

Change by Harold Klemp. I could certainly relate to this title since several recent dreams had involved tornadoes.

Scanning the back cover of the book, I noticed that the Holy Spirit was mentioned. That was all it took. I tucked it under my arm; noticing that my daughter was still busy, I continued my search. *Eckankar, Keys to the Secret Worlds,* by Paul Twitchell, was the second book that caught my attention. I was startled as I read the back cover. Chills ran up and down my spine as I realized that both books, even though they had been written by different authors, were about the Holy Spirit and a religious organization called Eckankar. I knew Spirit was up to something, and I became very excited as I anticipated my next spiritual assignment. It was these little adventures that gave some peace to my chaotic life.

I had been reading the new books for only a few weeks when, looking though a local newspaper, I noticed a lecture on dreams (which Brenda and I had been studying together) being given by the very name of the organization mentioned in the books. I experienced both fear and disbelief. Eckankar was such a strange name for a religion, especially for someone who came from a very traditional religion. What a "coincidence" to find a group meeting right in my own town.

Even in the face of fear, Spirit definitely had my attention. It was obvious this was a planned coincidence—the Holy Spirit was up to something again and I was, once again, along for the ride. By now I knew better than to even think about refusing an invitation, no matter what it was. I attended the meeting, not knowing if it was an occult religion or what. I jokingly gave my husband the address given in the ad, just in case I didn't return home. If he only knew how fearfully serious I was. This was another one of those turning points in life.

As I read more and more books by these authors, I couldn't find anything to disagree with and they answered a lot of my questions. Often, I didn't know I had the question until I found the answer.

If you think that the Holy Spirit coincidences were interesting—hang on! We are going from full screen viewing to high definition. Move over Linda, as Brenda makes her entrance.

Although Brenda and I had grown closer together since my divorce, I still hesitated to share these books with her. I thought they might be a little too far-out for her. She seemed to have more of a personal relationship with Jesus, whereas mine was with the Holy Spirit. Most of our time together was talking on the phone about our dreams and how to interpret them. Attending our annual family reunions had become a real joy since that was the only time we actually saw each other.

After about a month of reading these books, I could not hold it in any longer and decided to share my findings. Since their teachings revolved around dream interpretation as a way of spiritual guidance, I thought this would pique her interest.

I gathered my courage to present this new concept to her. To my surprise, she replied rather humorously, "Where have you been? I started reading their books a year ago." Interestingly, a friend had found them in the library and suggested she read them—"coincidently," one of them was the same book I had read. She had read the first part of one of the books and stopped when it said that Jesus was wrong in saying that he was *the way.*

I had read the same book, and remembered exactly the place she mentioned, as it had also caught my attention. What prompted me to continue reading was my curiosity as to why Spirit had directly guided me to read these books. I mentioned to her that, later in the book, it explained that what Jesus really meant was that the path he followed was *the way*, not him personally—he was the *way-shower.*

He had no intention of setting up a church for people to worship him. The path of following your own inner guidance is *the way* to finding the *key to life.* This explains why he said that what he did, we can also do, and even more. This does not sound like someone who wants to be put on a pedestal. No guru says, "Come on up on my pedestal," or "You can become greater than I am." The real difference between Jesus and other way-showers is that he was the first to experience oneness with God, and then it was his job to show us the way. The way-showers prior to Jesus had experienced enlightenment, but it was Jesus who took it to the next level—oneness with God.

Well, whatever I said worked, she began reading the books again and we both joined Eckankar. We made some wonderful friends and enjoyed another opportunity for us to be together at their seminars.

We found it amazing how parallel our lives were as twins. One example was that even though we lived hundreds of miles apart, we both had Eckankar friends named Sue, Dan, and Fred. We both still refer to the spiritual truths that Spirit taught us during this segment of our journey, just as we refer to the truths from the Bible.

B ♫ What were the chances that both of us would find this "nonmainstream" religion at about the same time and both through library books? I hadn't mentioned these books to Linda as I figured they were too "woo woo" for her. It was obvious to both of us this was the next spiritual assignment.

In the information, I felt as if I had finally found some of the missing pieces of the Bible when it came to understanding the inner worlds, dreams, soul travel, and reincarnation.

By this time, I too had meticulously searched my Bible for Jesus' true message, which led me to the importance of the Holy Spirit and that He was the way-shower, not the way.

When God Says It's Time for Change
—Then Listening Can Become Painful

L♫ In about the ninth year of our Eckankar study, I began to observe an interesting phenomenon. Up until then I had been in sync with their monthly spiritual lessons. For nine years, my personal lessons with the Holy Spirit had coincided with the lessons I received from Eckankar. Spirit brought dreams and life experiences based on that month's lesson. I began to notice that when I received my monthly lesson, I had already experienced it from the school of life. This took the excitement out of receiving my lessons. Now, Spirit's lessons had speeded up to the point that my lessons from Eckankar were several months behind. It was no longer the *Living Code* that I had looked forward to each month.

Once again, Brenda and I had both dedicated ourselves to an organized religion. But, just as the Holy Spirit had led us out of our childhood religion, it was now time to *take the next step* that lay beyond the teachings of Eckankar. Sadness came over us when we realized where Spirit was leading us because we would also be leaving our close spiritual friends. We remember very clearly pondering our inner question, *"What's beyond Eckankar?"*

B ♫ I remember, at one of their seminars, an Eckankar spiritual leader saying that there was always another step on the spiritual path—always something beyond where you currently are.

At this same time, I began to notice that some of the key people that had been on this path for many years were now leaving. I pondered how this could be and what they might know that I didn't. This activated my Taurus persistence and the quest began—what's beyond Eckankar? My inquiring mind wanted to know! The answers began to arrive, and once more I was at a spiritual crossroads, and knew the only choice was to follow the Holy Spirit.

"You Have Arrived" When Spirit Becomes Your Only GURU

L ♫ In the fall of 1998 I left Eckankar. Within a few months Brenda left also. (B ♫ Since she was born first it was her job to lead the way.) I was just doing my job—somebody had to do it! LOL

Of all our spiritual friends, we missed the ones in Eckankar the most, but we knew we had to leave organized religion. We were now literally on our own—

Spirit was now our only GURU!

What Hinders Us From Being a Good Receiver?

We cannot talk and listen at the same time. Reducing the mind chatter is a good place to start when learning to listen inwardly. There is so much we can learn by observing our conversational habits.

My motto is: *one ear inward—one ear outward.* This means you are 50% tuned inward and 50% tuned outward—*in the world but not of the world.* This is hard to do if you are talking—it is impossible if you are doing *all* the talking. *God talks in the silence as well as in the sound.* If you catch the subtle messages and follow them, then you won't have to hear the loud ones—the cosmic 2x4.

As a minister's wife, talking came with the territory—or so I thought. Eventually, I found myself talking nonstop when around other people. I sensed uneasiness with silence in a conversation, so my mind was always searching for something to say.

In my late twenties, I had a wonderful, painful awakening. I was riding in the car with my older brother and being my usual chatterbox. Very politely he said, "Why do you have to talk all the time?" Of course, my first reaction was shock and hurt feelings, but he certainly got my attention.

I began to observe my conversational habits. Finally, I had to admit to myself that he was right. That was another pivotal point in my life. Not until I was aware of my habits (self-knowledge) could I make changes. I soon became aware of how uncomfortable I was with silence when others were around.

As I began to listen to my side of the conversation, I made several observations. Did what I say have any value, or was I just talking to hear myself talk? Finally I realized most people are more interested in talking about themselves. I would challenge myself to have a conversation with someone where I did not mention the word "I."

When I was practicing this discipline, I received another challenge. In a conversation, I started a sentence and then received an inner nudge to not talk about the topic I had begun. In mid-stream I had to quickly change the ending of the sentence to a different topic—marveling that they did not notice what I had just done. Eventually, I would get a gut feeling that prompted me to change the topic *before* I started to talk about it.

B ♫ I, too, was uncomfortable with silence and wondered if it had something to do with my childhood programming: children were to be seen and not heard. As an adult, this prompted non-stop talking which was mostly about me. My awakening to this pattern started when, after several conversations with others, I realized I knew little about them or their "story" because the conversation had been all about me. I was a little embarrassed and promised myself to catch it sooner the next time.

Another awareness came with a couple of friends who constantly talked about themselves, giving meaningless details about people and events I didn't know and had little interest in. They were like a reflective mirror. When someone asked me the time, I would tell them how to build the clock. I also realized that when you are a non-stop talker you often, unknowingly, take energy from others. I had noticed that my friends, who were chatterboxes, were always full of energy. I also observed that after our conversations, I always felt drained of energy and had to work at not feeling guilty when wanting to avoid them in the future.

As I learned to be more comfortable with silence and began to meditate more, I realized a wonderful gift. God was in the gap, the silent space between the inhale and the exhale, simply waiting all this time for me to shut up.

Try Some Fun Stuff—A Little Self-Knowledge Goes a Long Way

L ♫ Notice the next time you are in a strong emotional conversation if you are half listening to them, because you are thinking of your next reply. Try to stop yourself from being sucked into their mental thought stream. You will find, as I did, that it is like trying to stop a runaway horse, which is almost impossible. Don't feel too bad if this takes a while to master. Even today, I'm on my guard when someone begins to express an emotional opinion. The bottom line is, "Who really cares?" It's just an opinion—their *story*!

The next time you are engaged in conversation, have a little fun and try a few of these suggestions just to get a feel for your conversational habits. No self-judgments allowed! All you are doing, for now, is stepping back and watching yourself in conversation. The fun part is that no one will probably notice what you are doing except you.

Become the Observer by listening to your spoken words!

1. Who does most of the talking in a conversation?
2. Who does most of the listening?
3. Who is the conversation usually about—yourself, others, ideas, or events?
4. Do your conversations empower or dis-empower—yourself, others, or ideas?

Now try this:

1. Try talking to someone without saying the word "I."
2. Engage in a conversation without mentioning yourself.
3. Try to emotionally detach from an emotional conversation. (You might find you have nothing to say.)
4. Try not giving your opinion unless it is asked for.
5. Ask inwardly before you speak: is this true, necessary, or kind?

Now, what did you observe about yourself? Be honest and take a good look at your conversation habits—remember no one is keeping tabs. Without judging—what did you observe?

From my experience, the one thing I can control is my talking—thoughts are harder to control. Talking was easier to control, once I became the observer of my conversations.

The main point is that when you talk to God, God talks back—learning to listen for the next step becomes vital. This is addressed in the next two chapters.

What Happens When You Do Not Want to Listen?

In the early stages of learning to listen, I remember only two times when I did not listen to the very strong voice that was giving me loud messages in my head. I paid the price for not listening (I almost lost a business over it), but I also learned the sound of that voice. From then on, regardless of what others thought or said about what I was doing, I followed my IGS. I learned that this inner guidance always had my best interest at heart, regardless of outer appearances. More than once I was asked to walk by faith.

B ♫ My inner listening skills developed in quantum leaps when I began to pay attention and listen to the messages given in my dreams. Listening to this form of *The Living Code* became the most powerful thing I did for my spiritual growth in the beginning years. In the next chapter, we will continue exploring some of the many ways God talks to us today by waking up to the world of dreams.

Chapter 4

WAKING UP TO THE WORLD OF DREAMS:

Blogging With God

"When you dream, all the scenery, characters, events, perils, and outcomes are built from your own consciousness, the darks and oppressions as well as the delights. Same with the world awake, though it takes you longer to build it."
— *Messiah's Handbook* by Richard Bach

By Brenda with Linda's ♫

I was excited when we discussed including a chapter on dreams because I had started the study and journaling of dreams over twenty-five years ago with the Edgar Cayce material. Since I already had much of this chapter written from years of notes and journals, the challenge was that of editing and condensing the volumes of information I had collected.

For both of us, the study and journaling of dreams connected us with a form of *The Living Code* that had been there all along just waiting to be deciphered. Dreams became a valuable communication tool in our quest for self-understanding; linking us to the kingdom within.

This study has been the most important and rewarding thing I did for my initial spiritual growth. Today, I relate to my dreams and subsequent personal journals, as being akin to "blogging with God/Holy Spirit"—an ongoing lifetime chronicle. These journals opened a doorway for spiritual communication, and the more I learned about dream interpretation, the more I received insightful messages from my Intuitive Guidance System (IGS).

Upon finding this valuable material, I was very hesitant to mention it to Linda because she was still in the family religious teaching that didn't acknowledge dreams. Finally, after her divorce, I mentioned my findings and was surprised at her receptivity. Apparently, her divorce created a shift in her way of thinking that now allowed her to be more open to concepts outside the box of our family religion. Sharing our dreams brought us closer together as we joined to find understanding in our daily lives. This was the initial instrument for Linda in opening the lines of communication with her IGS.

My husband Dave, who I lovingly call the "Dream Doctor," had already been teaching dream classes several years before we met, and in fact that was what brought us together. His dream class was more about the universal symbolic meaning of dreams and brought a new level of understanding to my more intuitive interpretations. I was excited when he finally decided to write an eBook, *Dream Logic—Waking up to the World of Dreams.*

This chapter is only *the tip of the iceberg* in the study of dream interpretation. A complete study would fill many volumes and is not the objective here. This chapter serves to give the reader a basic introduction to the universal symbols of the language of dreams and establishes the study and journaling of dreams as a valuable tool for spiritual guidance, helping us to navigate through the maze of our life experiences.

Dream Symbols are the Language of the Soul
—Allowing a Spiritual Course Correction

In Chapter two we mentioned that *the call* puts you in contact with the soul, and through dream interpretation we learn one avenue through which to speak the language of the soul. If you are willing to invest a little effort, practice, and persistence, the rewards are tremendous.

What a creative, loving gift to yourself when you learn to use dreams as a communication device to make a soul connection. It is exciting to know that within your very own consciousness you have a true friend who will always be there for you, tell you *the honest-to-God truth*, and will often use a lot of humor when you just need to lighten up.

Dreams serve as a universal language of the mind—a picture language of function. This language is based on how we view things in our waking life, but on a subconscious level. This allows us to more clearly identify, on a universal level, what our dreams are telling us. We often describe things in our life that reflect how this language works—*dream logic*: "Well, there's a mountain to climb," meaning we are facing a challenge or obstacle; "That's food for thought," or "Chew on that for a while," meaning food as knowledge for the mind to ponder.

Our unconscious aspect picks up buried perceptions and weaves them within the events of daily life. Learning some basic ways to look at our dreams will help break the code to discern their meaning. Dreams come to guide, help, and often use humor with puns and clichés. We are on the right track when we have an "aha, light bulb" moment about the possible meaning. Because of their deeply personal nature, the dreamer is the only one who can discern if the dream interpretation is true for them. It is helpful to take a playful attitude when interpreting a dream—make a game of it.

There is Order in the Chaos of the Dream World.

The more I studied and understood my dream symbols, the more my life made sense. I had developed a more intuitive style in my dream interpretation, and Dave's dream classes gave me a deeper understanding of the mechanics in applying the universal/mental aspect of interpretation. This was a valuable aspect for a fuller understanding of my dream symbols.

Dreams helped me to realize that I had to take responsibility for creating my own life experiences and were instrumental in helping me move out of the "victim hood" phase of life situations—a hard concept to accept, at first. Eventually, I learned to see life situations from a new perspective. When I understood the lessons held in my dreams and took action to change my thoughts and attitudes, my life began to change for the better. There were still many challenges, but now I had an avenue for help, and help was only a dream away.

As I studied my dreams with a true desire to learn, change, and apply the information to my daily life, my dreams also changed. When I learned that everyone in the dream represented an aspect of the dreamer on some level—conscious or unconscious—I stopped judging myself and others. At this point, my dreams began to show me things that I missed in daily life regarding how to deal with different personalities and situations.

The Twin Dreamers

In our dreams, we soon began to see a pattern, as we were often together and in school. At times, I would clearly recognize the subject of a new semester lesson and at other times Linda would get the subject of our lesson—quite often we both recognized them at the same time.

Usually, the themes were of us either starting school or graduating, which interestingly, often coincided with an actual physical school year—educational classes 24/7—the Holy Spirit by night, the personality ego by day, and one always fed the other. There were challenges to be faced when we couldn't seem to find our locker, our classroom, or at times, each other—even my anxiety about tests showed up in the dreams.

We loved the spring-time when the dream themes involved wedding ceremonies and graduations—sometimes high school and sometimes college. We enjoyed these dreams as they symbolized completions and new beginnings.

The Edgar Cayce material led me to my first book on the study of dream interpretation. *Dreams: Your Magic Mirror with interpretations of Edgar Cayce* by Elsie Sechrist, brought much valuable information. The author spent twenty years studying the complex relationships of dreams and based her work on the readings from the Edgar Cayce material. Sechrist felt that the moral standards of an individual are exactly reflected in the degree of clarity and quality of their dreams.

Sechrist related that Cayce felt that, if a person was seeking God's help, the Higher Consciousness would monitor his/her dreams. This would give them a clearer sense of direction in their daily life. He also felt there was little therapeutic value in simply learning the meaning of a dream unless an individual truly wanted to change or improve themselves.

The importance of dreams is definitely recorded throughout the history of Christianity. The Bible held many references indicating that dreams were a valuable communication channel between God and his people. As I began my study of dreams, I never quite understood why our family religion did not put any value on dreams. When I asked my mother about this, I received the same answer as I did for many other questions; "It only applies to those in the Bible, not us today."

The Value of Interpreting Dreams

1. As a reflection of our thoughts, attitudes, and emotions, dreams help identify patterns, give us honest feedback, and valuable help if we are willing to change. We can't change what we don't understand.

2. Since we are mental/emotional creators, they help identify how we are creating our life and identify thoughts that hold us back, enabling us to lead a more productive life.

3. They let us know when our life choices are on a positive track or have become sidetracked—both tracks are very necessary for spiritual growth.

4. Enables us to identify and become consciously aware of our positive and negative thoughts, feelings, and actions.

5. Information for healing on both physical and emotional levels.

6. Practical help in guidance for solutions in personal and business problems.

7. Encouragement, inspiration, and stimulation to bring out our more child-like creative nature.

8. Experience memories of other lifetimes or dimensions of reality—for self-knowledge and understanding.

9. Brings a depth of inner peace and comfort in knowing that valuable help with daily problems is only a dream away.

Basic Applications for Dream Interpretation

1. *Separate and identify the main symbols in the dream.* What is the relationship between the symbol and the action taking place? Pick out one or two key symbols that you understand and interpret those. Example: I was petting a cat or being attacked by one. The cat, if it is your own, would represent a familiar habit—animals are creatures of habit. Are you embracing a good habit or bad one?

2. *Look at the dream as a whole message.* Dreams process current events of our daily lives reflecting our recent thoughts and attitudes, and can be the result of personal fears and phobias. What is the overall feeling, tone, and theme of the dream? Pay attention to the emotions displayed in the dream as they can mirror our waking

life; calm or afraid, happy or sad, frustrated or angry. This is an indicator of how we are approaching or creating our life at this particuar time. Did the dream theme revolve around weddings, funerals, births, being chased, being in school, or other events?

3. Dreams can **remind us of something we failed to acknowledge or act upon** from our daily life. Look at dreams from a literal meaning. Watch for warning signs, objective truth, or reminders before going to the symbolic meaning. One dream warned me of a flat tire and within two weeks one of my tires started losing air. Another dream reminded me I had failed to act upon a spiritual assignment during my participation in Oprah's Internet book club class in 2008 on *The New Earth*, with Eckhart Tolle. This book spoke to my soul like a beacon in the night, guiding me home. When Oprah suggested rereading the book during the summer, I knew this was also my assignment but had gotten distracted with other life events. My dream, at this time, was of my teacher scolding me because I was behind on the assignment. The teacher was very annoyed at my getting distracted, so I apologized and knew what I had to do. Linda recognized it as her assignment too.

4. **Typically, every person in the dream represents an aspect of the dreamer.** Be honest in your self-analysis without self-judgment/beating yourself up, as the dream offers an opportunity for change. Look at one or two personality traits of the person in the dream and see how it might relate to your recent actions or thoughts. If your mother or ex-spouse is driving your car and you are a passenger,—have you been acting like them lately? How you relate to them tells you of positive or negative thoughts or actions. Who's in the driver's seat is an important message?

5. **Find the symbol in a dream book or make up your own.** The interpretation must feel right for you, or make up your own symbols and meaning as suggested by Elsie Sechrist. L ♫ By Brenda's recommendation, Sechrist's book was the first book I read on this topic. Her book helped me to learn my own dream symbols outside of the dream dictionaries. A good example is the symbol of an airport.

At the time, I had a business that involved frequent trips to the airport. Thus, airport dreams meant something entirely different to me (work) than the definition from a dream interpretation book (many choices of thoughts and ideas). This is a good example to show how closely the inner and outer realities are intertwined. A good dream dictionary: *In Your Dreams: The Ultimate Dream Dictionary* by Mary Summer Rain.

6. **Use children's playful way of interpreting life—free association.** This is one of my favorite ways to have fun while opening the intuitive nature. Let your mind wander; play with the possible symbolic meanings. Example: A two-year-old and I were in my flower garden; she looked at my gloves and said, "Bemba, I want some hands too." It was logical to her that gloves were just another set of hands. A friend told of his three year old granddaughter asking why he had cracks in his face. These young children can teach us much about dream logic with their very direct, innocent and refreshing approach in viewing life. Use this playful approach and watch your ability to interpret dreams soar to new heights.

7. **Sharing our dreams is important.** Linda and I enjoy sharing our dreams with each other and our husbands—*our dream partners*. Very often, new insights will come to mind during the process of sharing the dream experience with another. An ancient tradition with the indigenous tribes is to share their dreams upon wakening. They literally believe they live in two worlds; the physical and the dream worlds.

8. **The importance of journaling dreams.** This action helped me to become more of an observer of life's situations as I became aware of the themes in my dreams. These themes gave me a greater understanding of daily life events—the bigger picture. For many years, at the end of each month, I would make a summary page of the key topics for the month in the back of my dream journal. I always found it interesting that many themes repeated themselves during a several-week period. Some themes would be about going to school, weddings, births, funerals, and even bathroom dreams— all having great value.

9. *When writing or sharing dreams, watch for clichés.*

L ♫ This happened to me often. In one dream I was walking on an old country bridge made out of wooden planks—*walking the plank*. I was *on the edge* of the bridge while holding a five pound bag of sugar—carrying extra weight. I almost lost my balance. The clichés helped me interpret my dream; if I didn't stop eating sugar I would gain weight and be on the edge of possibly losing my physical health—my balance.

B ♫ In 2006 I had been overworking, stopped meditating, and life in general was frantic. In a dream I saw two trains heading toward each other. On one of them was a child shaking hands with an arm extended from the passenger car behind. The two trains collided and, after the crash, all I saw from the wreckage was an arm and a leg, knowing they had been severed. Dreams often embellish things to make a point. Upon waking, I knew the dream was urgently telling me that if I didn't slow down my mind and, thus, my life, it would cost me *an arm and a leg*.

Basic Keys for Dream Interpretation

1. Have a sincere desire to learn the process of dream interpretation and set an intention to do so daily.
2. Find a good dream book. Keep in mind that all dreams books are not created equal. Ask for help from your Inner Guidance System and the perfect one will show up.
3. Learning just a few basic dream symbols will get you started quickly.
4. Before bed every night, suggest to yourself that you will remember your dreams.
5. Keep a tablet and pen beside your bed to record dreams upon waking.
6. If you don't understand the dream, ask that it be repeated more clearly.
7. When you have a problem, ask for a dream of guidance. How many times do we wake up knowing the answer to our problems? Elias Howe, like many inventors, received a dream telling him where to put the eye in the sewing machine needle. I have an acquaintance

who takes a nap when she has a problem, knowing that the solution will be there when she awakens. Focusing on the idea that dreams will help you solve any problem will get this concept into your belief system, and become a reality.

Types of Dreams:

Informational

The majority of us have this is the type of dream most of the time, and it reveals general everyday feedback from our life experiences. This is just our subconscious mind processing our daily life events, but this becomes informational once we began to study our dreams.

Repeated dreams and nightmares—Why dreams play reruns

Repeated dreams serve to get our attention and indicate a pattern of some type of thinking that needs to be changed. If we do not acknowledge the message in the dreams, they can become nightmares in a last-ditch effort to get our attention. On one occasion, apparently I had ignored my warning dreams and upon awakening I heard a crystal clear, male voice give me an important insight, vital to my well being.

The movie *Groundhog Day* is a great example. The main character continued to have the same déjà vu dream every night that kept him frozen on one day—Groundhog Day—until he realized that to get out of the repeated dream loop, he needed to change his outer thoughts and actions. Every day he had one more opportunity to change the way he looked at life, until he finally got it right…sound familiar? When he made the effort to become a better person, the dreams stopped. Like this movie, our dreams may play reruns in an effort to get our attention and, thus, a message we may be ignoring.

One lady, an emergency room nurse, came to Dave's dream class with a deep concern about the nightmares she had been having for years. In the dreams she would always see horrible mutilations. Dave explained this was a drastic symbol from her subconscious mind attempting to show her that she was extremely hard on herself—beating herself up. Her friend, sitting beside her, nodded in acknowledgement. After she understood this message and saw her own self-sabotaging pattern, the nightmares became less frequent. She learned to use the dreams as a barometer telling her when she needed to be more forgiving and loving toward herself.

Lucid

In lucid dreams you feel more alert and aware than in your waking life—very surreal. Flying dreams are of this nature. Dreams where you know you are dreaming and can often change the outcome, could indicate that you have changed some thought or action that has put you more in control of your waking life.

In a lucid falling dream, I actually willed myself back up to the top of the cliff, which indicated I was exercising more control over my outer life circumstances. In another falling dream, I actually fell to the ground and saw and felt my spirit lift up out of my body. In the dream I realized I didn't really die, and this awareness helped me to begin releasing the fear of dying.

One exercise for lucid dreams is to frequently ask this question during the day: "Is this a dream?" Since we usually dream about familiar activities, the more often we ask the question, the more likely it will carry over into our sleeping state. Dave tends to have lucid dreams after listening to or reading some spiritual material.

Precognitive

Dreams foretelling a possible future event often give guidance for life situations. Prophetic dreams were common in the Bible, indicating that our dreams are not restricted by space-and-time and, thus, can be about the past, present, or future. Today, Quantum Physics is helping us to better understand this concept. When something is important for me to know, I occasionally have precognitive dreams which have a different feel to them. This type of dream helps us pay attention and be more aware in our daily life, and in some circumstances help us make a better choice.

In one pre-cognitive dream, I had left my purse somewhere, and the dream showed me that I was not to worry about it as it would turn out okay. Within a few days, I was shopping in a department store and absentmindedly left my purse in the bathroom stall. I didn't even notice until I heard my name called over the loud speaker to come to the service desk. Immediately, I realized I didn't have my purse and knew what happened. I started to panic, but then I recalled the dream and, sure enough, nothing was gone from my purse. Since I do not take from others, nothing was taken from me—a miracle in action—good karma at work!

Past-Life Dreams

Since I didn't always hold the belief in past lives, it took a while for me to recognize these types of dreams. If the clothing and dream setting are from another period of history, you are most likely dreaming of a past life. This has been a valuable avenue for me in explaining many of my relationships. Learn from the dream by paying attention to any details: the location, if anyone reminded you of someone in your life today, or how the activities relate to your current life.

In one dream, I saw myself as a male who had died in an accident because I was intoxicated. I had wasted a lifetime and learned a lesson. This explained my choosing to be born into a family where all drinking was viewed as a sin. I did not take my first drink until after I was married. It further explained why, in my twenties, I had an ability to drink in moderation—always, there was a small voice inside telling me when to stop. Today, I have very little interest in alcohol.

Dreams of England, Scotland, and Ireland told me why I always felt drawn to those countries. In another dream I was a black slave girl. My owner was my mother in this lifetime. Another dream told me that I had been owned by my ex-husband. These dreams told me volumes about these relationships—you have no power to express an opinion or say "no" to your owner. The dream information also helped me understand the heavy karmic debt I was balancing. This was a paradox in that these were the very circumstances I needed to awaken to my spiritual path.

Dreams of guidance and help

I often get dreams of guidance, especially when I am falling back into an old habit. The dream will often embellish the symbols to get my attention.

In one dream I saw a small globe-shaped shrub that held yellow apples. I understood that yellow apples were easier for me to digest than the red, more acidic ones. In another dream, a voice literally told me to, "stop wearing knee-high hose." I hadn't realized that because I wore them just below my knees, they blocked the circulation to my legs. I knew that wearing them on the calf of the leg was the solution.

In another, more bizarre dream in the late nineties, I found myself in a small one-seat, clear bubble-top hybrid car. It was urgent that I stop immediately and refuel from an alternative source. Upon awaking, I knew that I needed to take immediate action. I had been overworking and, thus, breathing shallowly—I was low on energy. The car represented my physical body, and adding fuel to a car to give it energy is symbolic of giving energy to our bodies through proper breathing—supplying oxygen, or energy, to our blood. Since the car was a hybrid, I knew I needed to add an alternative fuel/energy supply.

When I discussed this dream with Dave, he offered me a small book that held the answer. *The Science of Breath*, by Yogi Ramacharaka taught me the importance of prana breathing, which is vital to our life-force energy supply and different from regular air. Another confirmation for the dream information came shortly thereafter, when someone mentioned that by taking fifty deep breaths during the day your energy level would increase, and it worked. I could see how my outer life was working in harmony with my dream life.

Warning dreams and help from a deceased loved one

A friend and client lost her only sibling several years ago, a brother who was only twenty-six. He came to her in a dream with life-saving help. In the dream, she walked into a dark room and the only light was coming from a TV set across the room, which displayed a white static screen. Her brother was sitting to her right, in a recliner. All she could see of him was his left hand, the left side of his face, and a long-sleeved shirt. She noticed that the texture of his hand and face was red and bumpy, as if it had been burned. In her mind she heard him say, "Something is wrong with your stomach and you need to go to the doctor, don't put it off, everything will be okay." As the dream ended, she put her hand on her stomach and felt a sense of urgency.

She went to the emergency room and, knowing they would pay no attention if she told them she was there because of a dream, she embellished her symptoms to get their attention. The emergency room scans showed nothing. They sent her to an internist and found nothing, and then to a colon specialist at the Mayo Clinic, who found a rare kind of slow-growing, cancerous tumor on her intestine.

For this examination she was given the usual, required anesthesia but, oddly, she woke up twice during the procedure. The first time she saw a TV monitor with a white static screen, just as in the dream. The second time, the TV showed what the doctor said was her tumor…it was red and bumpy, just like her brother's face and hand in her dream. The doctors couldn't understand why she had awakened during the procedure.

This experience served as a valuable turning point for her spiritual life. Because she listened to the warning in her dream, she is healthy and cancer free. The subconscious used her deceased brother in the dream because it knew she would pay attention to him and, thus, have the courage and advice she needed to save her life. We truly are not alone; those on the other side are merely in another frequency/dimension of existence and can communicate and offer a helping hand, like a guardian angel.

Common Universal Dream Symbols—the Basics to Get You Started

Animals—compulsive or habitual ways of thinking or actions; your own pet is a familiar habit or compulsion. For animal symbology information we often refer to the book, *Animal-Speak.*

Bathroom—releasing and cleansing are needed. If you can't find one, you may be having trouble letting go of something you need to release.

Bicycle—balance in life experiences; are you in the ditch or on the path?

Birth, Babies, pregnant—new beginning, giving birth to new ideas.

Bridge—a means of transitioning from one point to another in life experiences.

Car—physical body; what is its condition? Is someone with you? Taken literally, can be a warning about your actual car.

Church—way of thinking, mind, specifically spirituality.

Chased—not wanting to see or face something in our daily life.

Death/funeral—change, completions, or endings.

Fire—expansion and cleansing.

Food—knowledge.

Gun, Knife—tool for causing change.

House—mind. Check the condition of each room or level.

Basement—unconscious thoughts.

Bathroom—condition of mind for purifying and cleansing.

Kitchen—condition of mind where knowledge is available.

Upstairs—the Higher Self.

Marriage/weddings—commitment or union.

Money—value, coins, a change or value.

Naked—openness and honesty; depending on how you felt about the nudity tells of your thoughts and feelings. Did you feel exposed because you shared a part of yourself that you usually hide?

People—aspects of self; think of two or three things you like or dislike about the person.

Police or military—discipline.

Road—path in life toward goal; is your road free of obstacles, what is its condition?

School—place for learning.

Sexual dreams—Harmony within the self regarding a creative endeavor, or a change in attitude or thoughts.

Storm or tornado—turbulent thoughts, inner emotional or mental turmoil.

Teeth—means of assimilating knowledge (food).Missing or loose teeth; unable to assimilate knowledge. "Chew on that for a while."

Test—need to access what has been learned. Being late for a class or test-not accessing what has been learned. Notice feelings about the test, anxious or unprepared?

Water—conscious life experiences or spiritual flow-living waters.

Ice, snow—unchanging conscious life experiences. Frigid thinking.

Row, Row, Row Your Boat Gently Down the Stream
—Life is But a DREAM

I always found it interesting that most of us sang this little song growing up, and it might very well define how life really works. Sages of old have alluded to this concept, and quantum scientists today are helping us understand that life, indeed, might be more of a dreamlike quality than what we call "reality." It depends on our focus. As we mentioned before, we do not see with our eyes, but with our mind/thoughts/belief system. Linda and I have had several experiences that helped us understand this concept.

In the 1980's, I had a profound dream experience on this very topic that provided many insights. In the dream, I saw myself with a teacher, a person so familiar that I didn't even look at him. He showed me a scene, like watching a play, only it felt like the fabric of a real life experience. I felt myself being pulled into the dream like experience, and in a short time, I was back with my teacher. He asked me what I had learned from the experience; I reviewed it and realized the lesson and how it applied to my daily life.

This experience clearly taught me how important the dream state is as a tool for understanding ourselves—self-knowledge, and thus, spiritual growth.

Ponderisms:
- ➤ If we learned the lesson in our dream could we then avoid a challenging experience in our waking life?
- ➤ Are we really just making (dreaming) this all up as we go along?
- ➤ If life is but a dream, where does one dream end and the other begin?
- ➤ What if our dreams, both night and day, are valuable tools to help us awaken, in safe increments, to our True Nature?
- ➤ What if life, is simply made up of different scenarios in chronological order, and given as opportunities to understand a spiritual lesson?

In the next chapter we will discuss taking the Dream World into the Waking World giving us a 24/7 Instant Messenger.

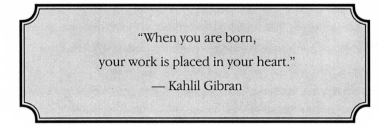

"When you are born,
your work is placed in your heart."

— Kahlil Gibran

Chapter 5

WAKING DREAMS

The 24/7 Instant Messenger

"If mankind were truly aware of the ephemeral nature of the world of forms, the way they approach daily life would be very different because external events also represent broader inner realities. Symbols contain a synthesis of timeless realities; therefore they transcend the chronology of the material world."
Mystery of the Cross in the Present Planetary Transition
— Trigueirinho

By Brenda with Linda's ♫

Words are not our teacher; life experience is our teacher.

Symbols, signs, and pictograms are forms of language used for communication, beginning with ancient civilizations. The Egyptians and the indigenous people believed that their symbols held the essence of the forces and energies that governed the universe. They also believed that every life experience held a deep secret meaning. They also knew that every number, word, picture—has a "vibrational frequency."

The Bible is full of references of signs and symbols. *For he is the living God who endures forever; He performs signs and wonders in the heavens and on the earth.* [Paraphrased] In Genesis, God gave the sign of a rainbow as one method of communication to all life on the earth; this one example explains how symbols energetically convey a complete idea or concept.

Airports and travel guides are great examples of the universal language of signs because they cross the cultural barriers. These are a small example of the ocean of symbols in which we live.

In the *Secret Language of Signs*, Denise Linn explains that signs have two basic functions. They can give us messages about our future and are messengers of important information about our current life situation because they act as reflections, telling us where we are in our life's journey.

Our waking life, like our dream life, also holds direct symbolic messages from our Intuitive Guidance System, waiting to be deciphered. As such, it seems appropriate to call our daily, waking life messages *waking-dreams*. We have 24/7 help, literally *at our finger tips*. Just as in our sleeping dreams, they are a communication tool between the inner level of spirit and the outer level of form, serving to build a bridge between the spiritual and physical realities.

It was an exciting turning point in my spiritual life when I realized that my dream symbols were much the same for my waking life, and I no longer had to go to sleep to get help—another avenue for spiritual communication. I no longer had to depend only on my dreams for help and guidance from my Inner Guidance System.

It is not uncommon in our classes on *Waking up to the World of Dreams and Waking Dreams* to have people who are searching for ways to recall their dreams. If you are one who does not remember your dreams; this chapter is especially for you.

Waking-dream symbols/signs are a language of function on the level of form. These encoded clues help us remember who we are and how to return home to God by learning to live from the heart—our access point to the kingdom within. As such, once we understand how to decipher the codes—*waking-dream logic*—they can give us daily guidance and help us make decisions that are in alignment with our soul's purpose. Waking-dreams help open and strengthen our intuitive nature; our connection to the Universal Source we call God.

My Initial Awareness of Waking-Dreams

In the 1980's, after years of studying and journaling my dream symbols, and at the Holy Spirit's prompting, I began to realize I could use my knowledge of these symbols in waking life in a similar way. I learned to apply many of the basic applications of dream interpretation to waking-life symbols. I began to see life as a secret language, the living code waiting to be deciphered.

Watching for these messages helped me begin to look at life in a new way, which became fun, exciting, and, often, very humorous. When teaching one of my waking-dream classes, a student commented that this sounded like too much work. I understood what she meant as at first I, too, made it hard by trying to make everything have a symbolic meaning. Once I understood the symbology and the feeling that comes when it is a message of importance, I learned to relax and trust the process, thus, making it more fun and much easier. The end result of having a greater spiritual connection and growth has been well worth the time and effort.

Learning the Language of the Soul—Angel Messages

Like dreams, waking-dreams are one more avenue to learn the language of the soul. It is not learned through left-brain logic. To open the door for communication to the Spiritual worlds, you have to be willing to move out of the mind into that playful nature that only the heart knows. A valuable skill of life is learning how to balance the right and left brain functions—serious, intellectual mind and the intuitive, playful mind of the heart. We must learn to think with our true nature from the heart, which is the true balance of heart and mind.

The signs and symbols of waking-dream messages can also be thought of as *angel messages*—messengers from God. Our angels are not beings outside of us; they are a higher level/frequency of our soul's energetic essence. Making this connection is just a shift in our perception which is learning to live from the heart, and waking dreams can help us make the transition or shift to a more Spirit-led life.

Once in a while I talk with someone who is very frustrated and even angry because their angels don't communicate with them. As they explained this to me, I could see that they were coming from the left-brain logic, as frustration and anger closes the intuitive communication door. This is like traveling to a foreign country and getting upset because they don't speak your language. I usually ask these people what avenues of intuitive communication they are learning to help open the communication channels—to speak soul's language to make that *Soul Connection*.

Soul language is not about left-brain logical processing. In this chapter we will give many avenues for spiritual communication, helping you to make the journey out of the mind and into the heart. If you want to hear what your angels are saying, you must be willing to meet them halfway and learn at least a few avenues of communication to get the door open.

As with the last chapter on dreams, I had volumes of information from experiences, journals, and teaching classes on this subject for many years; again, condensing and editing was the challenge. This chapter, too, is only the *tip of the iceberg* in the study of waking-dreams. We will explore many different techniques you can use to interpret the symbolic messages in your waking life. From this context, we might think of life as one big reflective mirror, as our present-moment awareness reflects back to us this pivotal point where the inner and outer realities meet.

This is not new information

Today, many people are aware that the synchronicity and coincidences in their lives have meaning. Our goal is to give you, the reader, user-friendly techniques to get you started or to enhance your own developing system to interpret personal signs and symbols. We wish to strengthen and rekindle the "joy of being" the observer of life and the never-ending opportunity for spiritual communication, guidance, and growth. Learning this simple, basic language is more important today than ever before because of the many challenges we all face.

As in the symbolic language of our dreams, our waking-life symbols can also mean something different because of our cultural, religious, and historical backgrounds. An example is the symbol of a snake. In some cultures, it might be a warning of deception, "a snake in the grass," while other cultures view it as a spiritual symbol for transmutation, wholeness, and healing, as in the physicians' caduceus. We might even be drawn to symbols from past lives when we feel drawn to travel to foreign countries or decorate our homes in a certain cultural style. My pull toward other cultural items/symbols reflect lifetimes in England, Egypt, and as a Native American.

Ponderism: *In the realm of messages from signs and symbols, do day-dreams, night-dreams, and waking-dreams all have relevance—like cohesive partners?*

Waking-Dreams—Insight Into the Spiritual Nature of the Present Moment

When you sincerely want to know something and you are in that place of allowing, the Universe always responds. There are, at all times in your present moment experience, 20, 30, 40, 100, 1,000 synchronistic signs ready to pop, right now, into your experience because you are in vibrational alignment with them. [Paraphrased] The Teachings of Abraham ™

Waking-dreams help us understand that every moment truly is a spiritual moment. When we have our Watcher "tuned-in and turned-on," waking-dreams become *present-moment tools*, reflecting our thoughts, feelings, and actions back to us.

This valuable "present-moment" guidance gives us insights for every detail of our lives, even decisions about the future. As avenues for communication with the spiritual realm, they are a confirmation that we are *never alone* and *always* have help.

They connect us with the eternal, present moment that we relate to as God's love. This present-moment connection allows us to line up with "miracle moments" through synchronistic events—if we are paying attention to the signs along the way. We are the Kingdom within and miracle moments are a result of our connection with our True Nature—our authentic Self. When they aren't happening in our lives, this is a sign that we are no longer traveling on the high-lighted path and, thus, are out of alignment with our True Self.

What We Focus on Expands
—Waking-Dreams are the Law of Attraction in Action

Today, many people are aware of this universal principle. The Universe/ Source Energy always gives you signs in relationship to your thoughts and feelings (your vibration), which is perfect feedback for what and where you are now, and who you have become. What we focus on, positive or negative, draws to us, a life reflecting this principle. Our daily symbols/signs appear as a result of our habitual thoughts and feelings.

If we focus more on waking-dreams, we will naturally notice more help from our Intuitive Guidance System. Even the Bible says that what a person thinks in their heart, they become. *When you begin to make the correlation between your thoughts and your life experiences, then you are empowered.*

At the beginning of each year, Linda and I ask for Divine Guidance to give us messages for the focus of the coming new year, which draws to us insightful dreams and waking-dreams. As the new year approaches, we begin to pay attention to our dreams and pull cards (like angel or animal cards), to help us connect with our intuition and thus the overtones of the coming year.

My cards for 2008 were *balance, nature,* and *abundance.* I thought the word nature was telling me to spend more time in my flower garden, "get back to nature." Then, a Wayne Dyer PBS special gave me another perspective when he mentioned that it was time to get back to our True Nature, our Divine Self. From then on I saw and heard the word "nature" many times—always referring to a Spiritual Nature; surprisingly, it was even on my new yoga DVD. By putting my focused attention on these words for the year, I had connected with the deeper spirit (understanding) of their meaning.

As I began to align with my True Nature by connecting with the environmental nature, the earth, this helped to bring *balance* and *abundance* into my life on many levels. As I spent more time with nature, meditation, and yoga exercises, my mind slowed down and so did my life. I stopped doing the things that I didn't enjoy, regardless of their financial support, and stopped feeling overwhelmed by my schedule.

To my surprise and delight, I had more time, energy, and money; I had tapped into the True Source of abundance, which helped to create a beautiful relationship with all of them. My life still requires monitoring, lest I fall back into old habits, but I can now rely on my waking-dreams as well as my sleeping-dreams to keep me on the highlighted path back home to God.

CAUTION! If you read further you will never look at life the same again—proceed at your own risk!

Exploring Different Ways to Receive Messages—Signs

Ponderism: *How much control do we have over our waking-dreams, or do they merely happen by default?*

The process of deciphering the message is somewhat obscure and is easier taught by examples of experiences rather than explained with words. When trying to decipher the symbolic message of the experience, it is important to catch the feeling, which is the "spirit" of the message.

Waking-Dreams—Self-Activation or by Default?

At first, when Linda asked God to send signs her way, twice, as confirmation for her direction, she was unknowingly self-activating waking-dreams. When we make the *call for help*, by the Law of Attraction, Source Energy always responds and requires only that we trust the answer to come, and to stay alert for any clues that might come our way. Once we understand this as the mechanics of how we activate waking-dreams, we really open to a deeper awareness—the ocean of symbolic information we live in, and almost by default, a feather dropped on our path suddenly means something.

Self-Activated Signs—Indicator Symbols

These are fun and easy. When you have a "heart felt" question or decision to make, you can ask for a specific sign to appear as confirmation for timing and direction. This is a great tool to practice being present and a confirmation that when you ask, the Universe/God delivers.

You can also ask for immediate answers—the Instant Messenger—when you need answers to imminent questions. I had this opportunity when a friend called me really concerned about the economic banking problems. Her study of astrology had suggested that some real problems could come up within the next few days. She was suggesting that to be on the safe side, I might want to pull some money out of the bank.

I hadn't really gotten any nudges in this direction, but my "girl scout" instinct wanted to be prepared—I didn't have a lot of money in the bank and I needed what I had. I was about to leave work, so I emphatically asked Spirit to please give me a sign before I arrived home and that would be in just seven minutes! I had made too many choices coming from fear and none of them were correct, now I wanted to know my heart-thoughts about this decision.

As I drove home, I began to notice that a small green truck kept riding my bumper. I could feel his "rushing energy" wanting to speed ahead as he moved into the next lane and then back behind me again. He couldn't get around me because a full-sized green truck was driving beside at the same speed. I don't usually experience vehicles riding my bumper, so I knew to pay attention. Both trucks were the color of money. I couldn't recall ever having seen this bright green color on a truck, and now there were two of them.

I quickly pondered the meaning and clearly felt the message was to not let anyone's fears cause me to rush into a decision—stay at your steady pace. I had my answer and, sure enough, nothing happened regarding the banks that affected my finances.

I did learn an important aspect to walking dreams with this experience. I had never given Spirit a deadline before and this almost felt sacrilegious, but I felt desperate for help and was delighted and surprised, to have the answer arrive so quickly. I pondered the mechanics of this event and it seemed that my urgent, heart felt plea for help had somehow activated a strong energy that produced a reply so quickly. Could it be that the reply returned with the same conviction with which the request was made? I was also writing this chapter at the time and maybe Spirit had a hidden agenda to get a good point across. We do have immediate access for Divine Guidance and no request is too small. How cool is that!

The White Feather Symbol

My love for spiritual writing started when I began to notice the waking-dreams. The idea of a book always simmered on a *back burner* in my mind, but finding the time, energy, and finances made it a challenge. I love feathers and decided to set up a self-activation sign that, when white feathers started appearing, that was my cue to make the commitment to start writing.

In 2005, a friend sent me a small thank you note with a picture of a little girl with white wings (feathers) at a writing desk. I made a mental note. Within a few days, my niece, who loved to walk at a local duck pond, brought me a beautiful little white feather that looked just like a writing plume. In a few weeks, at Christmas, a friend gave me the gift of a beautiful, transparent tree ornament that she had made. A white feather was inside the ball, and a small tag that said: "Give thanks to those above for answering your call."

I didn't feel I had the time to write a whole book, but I could write spiritual short stories from the messages I was receiving in my dreams and waking-dream experiences. The process was fun and more like a spiritual puzzle as the pieces would come to me from any source, at various times—day and night. I was even given the name of these short stories: *Ponderisms—Potent Points To Ponder—Spiritual Insights for Daily Living.* This was like blogging with God and so www.bloggingwithgod.com was born. At the end of this chapter is one of my first stories.

Quick Keys for Deciphering Messages

When you recognize something as a waking dream, check your immediate thoughts to see if they are in sync; if the meaning isn't immediately evident, check the present focus of your life.

- Unusual events
- Free association—check for a literal meaning or a symbolic one
- Words that jump out at you—*out of the blue* or from a *slip of the tongue*
- Physical symbols or signs repeated until they get your attention
- Something will keep coming to mind until you acknowledge the message
- Physical chill bumps or tingles are confirmations
- Discussing your messages with someone often brings more insights

The more you can learn about the symbolic meaning of things, the more avenues you give Spirit for direct communication. I was guided to learn numerology, Native American animal signs, and Ancient Runes. My intuitive soul symbol paintings taught me much about ancient and sacred geometry symbols. Below, we will explore messages in everyday life experiences: songs, billboards, TV, radio, license plates, animals, numbers, and seemingly simple life events.

Some messages are very subtle, like a whisper carried by a gentle breeze and placed in your heart, a soulful message that continues to play in your mind until acknowledged. Some of mine have been so persistent that I took the action required, just to get them to stop playing in my head. This, of course, was their point—moving me past my resistance.

These whispered messages are easier to capture when our conscious mind is off-guard. When we meditate or pray to refresh and renew our mind, we can more readily hear them. We can also hear them when we are performing mundane activities—ironing, doing dishes, or driving on a long stretch of highway—we actually shift into a relaxed, altered state. This relaxed and open state creates a stronger bond with our intuition.

If you have difficulty understanding the message received, let it go and ask for a clearer sign. Do not stop and analyze every detail of your daily life, which would be work. Make an agreement with Spirit to let you know when something is a message of guidance. With practice, you will learn to recognize the difference between a Spirit-guided message and a personality-ego message. Once you learn the basics, you move into a flow that is creative, exciting, and fun. There is often a humorous pun involved and a good chuckle always helps to lighten the spirit.

Unusual Events—the Frog and the Lemon

Always look for a deeper message when you find yourself saying, "What are the chances of that happening again?" There are no accidents. These messages have a specific purpose, like a shock treatment bringing you into present-moment awareness. We might look at them as *mini-wakeup moments*. Combining the event with your immediate thoughts or the theme of your thoughts of the day will give the sign more relevance. The following stories will help you understand this concept.

Upon leaving my office building one day, as I put my hand on the push-bar to open one of the large double-glass doors, my attention was drawn to the two metal pull-handles on the opposite side of the doors. It is not my habit to look at these handles upon exiting, so I was startled to see what was attracting me. What a surprise to see a good-sized frog balanced on the top of the handles! My first thought was, "What were the chances of that happening again?" I left through another door to my right and helped the frog to safety, but I made a mental note of the incident. From there, I went to a store where, immediately, my attention was pulled to a counter-top display of frog key chains made of bright green cloth.

From my study of Native American symbols, I knew that frogs meant emotional cleansing and transformation. I related this to the emotional clearing exercises (see chapter nine) I had been doing regarding the fear of my work not being good enough, while writing this chapter. The frog on the door handle was telling me about this emotional cleansing and that, "I had a handle on it." Gratefully, my dreams also confirmed this.

When Dave and I were looking for a house to buy, we always previewed the neighborhood and exterior of the home before calling the realtor and were excited about one particular property. On the way home, at a stop-light, a small truck pulling a flat-bed trailer crossed in front of us. On the flat-bed was an unusual object—a lemon the size of a Volkswagen, and it was headed in the direction of the house we had just looked at. We looked at each other and said, "What are the chances of that happening again?" We had a good laugh because the meaning was so obvious. The next day the realtor confirmed our message; the home was a disaster, and to top it off, it had the 1970's burnt orange and avocado green shag carpets—what a lemon.

In midsummer, Dave was mowing our front yard when he suddenly called to me. He was holding up a large baking potato that he found near the sidewalk. What are the chances of that happening again? In pondering this, we knew that something in front of us, in this case, our front yard, represented a present-moment situation. Dave and I know that nutrition is a key to feeling good and had begun to notice a reaction when eating too many starchy foods, like potatoes—we tossed the spuds out of our regular diet.

Dropping Something

When you drop something, check your immediate thoughts and if they are negative, "drop them." For no apparent reason, I have had items fly out of my hands.

One morning, I got a feeling that I needed to stop taking my daily ritual of a liquid supplement. As I put it back into the refrigerator I contemplated taking a smaller amount. This large new bottle literally flew out of my hands, landed on its top, breaking the cap and the liquid flew across the kitchen floor. Okay, that was clear! I stayed in gratitude for the help, as I cleaned up the sticky mess.

If you drop something that shatters, this could be a symbol that emotionally or physically you have just let something go—something shattered. When this happens I refrain from using negative self talk—"what a klutz." I immediately know something in my way of thinking or in my life has shifted. This understanding helps keep my focus on the positive side of life.

Is Life Tripping You Up?—Watch Your Thoughts!

The next time you find yourself walking and suddenly you stumble or trip for no apparent reason, stop and look at your immediate thoughts. Have you *stumbled onto something* important or is *something tripping you up*?

Early one morning, knowing I had a busy day ahead, I pondered the need to allow time for my yoga workout. Immediately, the toe of my right sandal caught on the carpet and I knew this was a confirmation—I had stumbled onto an important thought. The right side of the body symbolically represents the male energy to "take action" and a need to address something in a present situation.

Instant Messenger—First Impressions Do Matter!

Years after my divorce, I began to get messages on my answering machine from collection agencies demanding payment on my ex-husband's past debts. It was a threatening male voice saying this was my last chance to pay the debts, and that I had twenty-four hours to respond or suffer harsh consequences. Listening to the message, I could feel my heart pounding with fear and the dread of taking on one more of his part of the divorce debt. As difficult as it was to calm my fears, I had learned in these situations to quickly quiet my mind and ask for help. The calm inner voice replied, "Do nothing, this too shall pass." My "over-the-top" fear desperately wanted control of my emotions, and within minutes I even began to doubt the initial first impression of my guidance.

I began some positive affirmations, asking to perceive this in another way. Thirty minutes later as I was leaving for work, I asked for another *sign* from Spirit as confirmation of the message because as the caller suggested I had only a few hours to respond—or else!

My work was a short five-minute drive, so at a stop light I anxiously started looking around for any sign of confirmation. The Inner Voice said, "Stop, you are trying to make it happen—let it go." I knew I had to relax even though my office was only a couple of minutes away.

At the next red light, right in front of me I saw a city bus that had just pulled out of the pickup station. While waiting, I casually glanced at the large one-line advertisement covering the rear of the bus: *First Impressions do matter!* It was an ad for a *sign* company! I chuckled as I pondered the connection; to me the sign company was The Universal Sign Company—a sign from God. I see a city bus every morning at this stop and never again have I seen this one.

Over the next few months, fewer threatening calls occurred. With each call I was less reactive because I was continually clearing fearful emotions as they came up, using the exercises given in chapter nine. Information from other sources continually came my way confirming that the initial message was the best action—"Do nothing, this too shall pass."

Golden Tongue Wisdom—A New Way to Listen

As mentioned earlier, our Intuitive Guidance System speaks to us 24/7, if we learn to listen. Messages can come via any source of written or verbal communication. Words that seem to jump out at you from a *slip of the tongue* or *out of the blue* comments are usually messages. The other person may not even know why they said what they did, but you will, because it will address one of your current challenges or ponderings. *Always take your first impression* on what was read or said, as it may be different when reviewed again. The intense desire for help with a challenge can trigger an answer in this format.

One of Linda's experiences with the golden tongue wisdom helps us understand that no request is too small. She had a common seed wart on her toe and after several attempts to remove it, the wart was still there. Shortly thereafter, she met with a friend for lunch. In the middle of the conversation, out of the blue, her friend casually mentioned that the essential oil of lavender will remove these warts and then went on with her conversation without any further reference to what she had just said. Linda was able to remove the wart with this information thanks to the *Golden Tongue Wisdom*!

Words Jump Out At You

A sign that something is a message happens when written words seem to "jump off the page." Messages can arrive via junk mail, cards, newspaper headlines, billboards, etc.

A small button pin that Linda had given me lay on my vanity, with the words FOR MOR written on it. Daily, it kept pulling my attention. Free association and an intuitive feeling told me that there was *far more* to life than what I was experiencing. A few days later on my bank web site there was a new ad featuring a lime-green bicycle with the license plate as the focal point, which said, XPCT MOR. The bank also mailed a six-by-nine-inch card of the lime-green bike and, again, the focal point was the license plate, XPCT MOR. The fact that the letter "E" had been left off of MOR, on both of these, caught my attention. I knew I needed to raise my expectation because we do get what we expect in life—positive or negative.

Several months later my husband and I were in Hot Springs, Arkansas on vacation and visited a beautiful botanical garden. To my disbelief at the entrance of the garden on the bike rack stood a single bicycle. It was the actual lime green bike from the banks advertisement with the glaring license plate—XPCT MOR. Of course I took a picture and really held back the desire to ride it.

The Truck Driver's Message in the Land of Billboards

I gave a talk about waking-dreams to a singles group at a local church. The next week we went back for Dave to give a talk on dreams. A man who had been at my talk approached me and explained that he was a truck driver. He was recently divorced from a woman he still loved and even though it was not a harmonious relationship, he still wanted her back. After he attended the class, he was driving through New Jersey thinking about the situation when he looked up to see a billboard with these words, "Give it up." He knew, instantly, that it was a message regarding his immediate thoughts. He thanked me for helping him to realize that he needed to let go of the relationship.

Overhearing Conversations

This avenue for messages does not mean that you eavesdrop on other peoples' conversations. When it is a true message meant just for you, the words that are meant for you is all you will hear; the rest of the conversation will seem like white noise playing in the background.

Quite often, as I enter the health food store looking for a certain item, I *just happen* to hear another customer asking for that very item. Amused and grateful, I simply follow along to its location. Another example: while eating in a restaurant I overheard a lady at the next table mention that the Orchid Show was the next day. I wanted to attend this show but had forgotten about it. Because of the Golden Tongue Wisdom, I had a lovely time the next day, lost in the sea of beautiful orchids.

Television and Movies

These two avenues have carried so many messages for both of us. Years ago, at a time in my life when I was regretting some of the choices I had made and getting down on myself, the voice on the TV said, "That is what you did, it is not who you are."

When we began writing this book, the movie *Finding Forrester* with Sean Connery, pulled Linda's attention at a video store and, surprisingly, it held a major clue for our writing. The movie was about a young, aspiring writer who was told to write his first draft from the heart and the second draft from the mind. This was a much-needed reminder of an exercise we had learned years ago.

Another good TV show that we had a lot of fun sharing some really amazing spiritual insights was *Babylon 5*. One character completely transformed from a total war-monger role into a loving, compassionate being with great spiritual insights and strength. These writers, like many others who convey messages through this medium, connected with a higher spiritual truth with subtle messages for those who were paying attention.

Songs—Soul's Serenade

This is another favorite avenue for messages. Messages come from songs that keep coming to mind. Sometimes the words may be changed—go with your first impression. Many times I have awakened at 3:00 a.m. to have a song running through my mind. Some songs will stay with me for days. For example, as I was writing this chapter, I kept singing an adaptation of an old song: I'm having day dreams about night dreams in the middle of the afternoon. Maybe I was O.D.'ing on dreams.

One evening I was feeling sorry for myself—having a "pity-party" and this song kept playing in my mind, "I never promised you a rose garden, along with the sunshine there's gonna be a little rain sometime."

For a couple of years I have been finding beautiful little rocks in the shape of hearts, "heart rocks," whenever we go hiking and then I also began noticed songs about love were popping into my awareness at various times of the day and night. I knew these were messages about my learning to live from the heart, and I finally made the correlation between my thoughts and feelings. I knew I was moving into greater alignment with my True Nature— the sacred space in my heart. Some of the Songs that I knew related to God's love and held a special meaning for me: *"Love the 'One' You're With," "Your love keeps lifting me higher, than I've ever been lifted before," "Love IS All There Is."*

Help With Health

I met a friend for lunch and we ordered hot tea before our meal. I don't usually have caffeine drinks but, this time, I decided to throw caution to the wind. When the tea came, I looked at the package and something was covering the first letter of the name of the tea; all I saw was the word, "risk." Immediately, I thought about the caffeine being a risk; I know how it makes me feel. It occurred to me that I would be drinking this on an empty stomach, so I decided to wait and drink my tea with lunch. On closer examination, I discovered the name of the tea was Brisk Tea.

Additional Avenues for Waking-Dreams

Animals

Animals have been a major waking-dream resource for both of us. When you start seeing a certain animal from various sources, this is your que to research the symbolic meaning.

In the early 1990's our intuition guided us to two books about animals that were invaluable; *Animal Speak* and *Medicine Cards.* The book, *Medicine Cards* had companion cards. For a year, we pulled an animal card each day, studying the symbolic message of the animal. From this time on, animals began showing up in our lives with valuable messages.

The turtle shows up when I need to slow down, get grounded, and become more focused. The blue jay message is no fear; the cardinal is pay attention as an important event or message is coming; the butterfly means transformation, connecting with your angels, and intuition; the hawk is the messenger and protector and is always with us when driving. The crow shows up when I need to become truthful and introspective—*Caw it like it is.*

Numbers

For both of us, numerology has been another key avenue for Spiritual communication. Numbers hold a vibrational frequency. The numbers in our name describes our true nature and disposition also indicating our talents and potentials to understand our purpose for living.

We were well aware of the importance of numbers as indicated in our Bible. As we began to see their esoteric meaning, we recognized them as one of God's "tools" for communication. In 1987 we discovered a wonderful numerology book, *Numerology and The Divine Triangle* by Faith Javane and Dusty Bunker, which we continue to use today.

Because numbers are so prevalent in our world it is well worth the time and effort to learn the basics. It is as easy as memorizing two or three words relating to each number.

I began teaching numerology classes in the late 1990's. To demonstrate their usefulness, in class I asked a student to quickly give me the first three numbers that came to mind. These numbers told me what was going on in his life and emotions, just from using the basic information listed below. He was surprised at the accuracy of the information. This exercise is a lot of fun and very helpful in learning the science of numbers.

    1 - New beginnings, independent, courage
    2 - Cooperation, intuition, harmony, meditation, partnerships
    3 - Freedom, happy, scattered, inspiration, creative
    4 - Practicality, work, stable, sound reasoning
    5 - Adventure, change, travel, freedom
    6 - Service to others, family, love of home, artistic
    7 - Introspection, achievement, health issues, rest, most sacred number
    8 - Karma, power, money, business, executive ability, realist
    9 - Humanitarian, endings, introverted, intuitive
  10 - The God energy. The zero combined with any number is powerful.
  11 - Reflects the transformation of the physical into the Divine

Two or more of the same number, combined, are considered master numbers and carry more energy. A popular number for angel messages is 444, as referred to in the book *Healing With The Angels* by Dr. Doreen Virtue. My husband once asked for a confirmation that his guides/angels were with him and, that day he saw two 444 messages. Linda's husband, Tom, frequently watches the sun rise over the Eiffel Tower via a webcam that updates the view every ten seconds. On August 10, 2008, he noticed the date was stuck on 08-08-08 and the time was 17:07:07. He pondered that for a while!

License Plates—Excellent Source for Messages

Tom, is also an avid license plate watcher, especially the symbolic meaning of the numbers and repeated plates with the same numbers. Prior to moving to a new home, Tom kept seeing plates with the combination of three numbers—416, 614, etc. While at an intersection one day, he pointed out to Linda three cars with license plates imprinted with this mysterious combination of numbers.

A few days later, the mystery was solved when Linda called about a house listed in the paper. She knew immediately that this was the house for them when the man said the address was 416 Garland. As it turned out, it was perfect for their needs, especially since it was only one half-a-block from where Tom worked.

In the summer of 2004, for several weeks I noticed license plates with the last three letters spelling Amy. I knew it was a message. I had been pondering reading *A Course In Miracles;* it had come to my attention several times. I decided to call a used book store, thinking I could give it away if I didn't like it. The store had one hard-back copy and they would hold it for me.

The next morning I opened the front cover and noticed the prior owner had erased a penciled note that was still faintly readable: To Amy, A true seeker. Peace and Love, Will. Chills came over me when I made the connection to the license plates. I had also been pondering the right use of will-power in a spiritual context.

Linda and I had little difficulty understanding the workbook messages of the Course since our studies began years ago when the Holy Spirit entered our lives. The Course was a confirmation of the lessons that Spirit had given us. We enjoyed the refresher course of the daily meditations in the workbook lessons. This often brought memories of our past spiritual experiences while learning a particular lesson. It was exciting to now see the lessons in print.

Your Personal Vehicle

Vehicles are wonderful avenues in helping with waking dream symbols. Buying a new car can symbolize new beginnings, a new state of consciousness, or a new level of health. Vehicle problems: radiator overheats—Are you steamed up about something or are you letting off steam? Flat tire—Are you out of energy and need to stop and rest? Muffler problems—Are you being too chatty or do you need to muffle your opinion? Starter problems—How are you starting your day? Am I having trouble getting started for the day or starting a project? Battery problems—are you low on energy or do you need to recharge your battery by getting more rest.

The Great Escape—the Conscious Exit

B ♫ After twenty-six years, it became very clear that it was time to leave my "roller coaster ride" marriage that was filled with his explosive anger and my "poor me" victim role. I had done my forgiveness work for both him and me, knowing his anger was reflecting my own inner anger. My Watcher skills where now on, more than off, thanks to the help of Divine Spirit, and the many self-help books I had been nudged to read for many years. This spiritual attribute of observing life without judgment helped dissipate the loss of power I experienced in my marriage; more about this in chapter eight. For over a year, I had sent out heartfelt prayers for a way out of the relationship.

I had an inner knowing that the karmic debt was balanced because I no longer reacted to his anger episodes and control dramas. Leaving would be a big leap of faith since I would have no money, no job, and very few possessions; I was thankful for the guidance to go live with Linda—my saving grace. She was to come for a visit and help me pack and drive to her home.

Six months before my departure, I began to get the waking and sleeping dream signs. It was as if my intuitive inner ear was clear and open as, almost daily, I received simple, specific guidance for every step.

It all began on my way to work one morning when the large billboards lined along the entrance ramp onto the freeway were suddenly pulling my attention—my cue for a message. Their messages were: *Your deadline is closer than you think*, *Make new memories*, *Do you believe in magic?* This last one reminded me of a song that I had loved to sing, "Do you believe in magic in a young girl's heart?" For me, magic meant miracles. Then a license plate pulled my attention; it had my initials and three fives, my Destiny Number, which meant freedom, change, travel, and adventure. I also began to see billboards with these same messages all over town.

This was to be the biggest leap of faith I had ever taken. Only once did I fall into self-doubt and, immediately, another billboard appeared that was a cartoon drawing of a large funny-looking dog with big floppy ears, and in large letters the message was, *Don't get scared, get organized*. This told me to get my focus back on the goal and to stay organized, which was something that I did well. This shift in my focus helped me to stay out of fear. I had more courage than I had ever known.

Dreams and waking-dreams continued to guide me with very clear messages, in seemingly miraculous ways. I was given every detail regarding how and when to leave. I just had to stay present and pay attention.

It was very clear that I was to ship my personal things to Linda, make copies of all legal documents and bills, and not mention my departure to my husband until the end of the final day. A dream had revealed the plan for the "great escape." I was out of my victim role and did not have to stay for one more anger episode—this woman was now awake and aware. Who would have thought that I owed much of my spiritual growth and self-empowerment to this relationship?

After arriving at Linda's, my next prayer for help was in asking how to make this divorce a "win-win" situation for both of us. My pondering brought the intuitive knowing that I was to give him everything and this would also simplify the divorce. After a year of asking and waiting for messages about when to file the papers, I finally saw a billboard with these large words: *Call Your Lawyer*. I didn't even know who the sign was advertising and I never saw it again.

I had neither a lawyer or a lot of funds to pay for one, but thankfully Spirit was in charge and knew the plan. Within a week, one of Linda's customers, who "coincidentally" happened to be a lawyer, came into the alteration shop. Little did he know that he was a part of Spirit's plan for my divorce and for Linda's (nine months later), and the fee was well within our small budgets.

After leaving the courthouse on the day of my divorce, I sat in the car and gave a prayer of gratitude for all the help I had received. My heart was open in appreciation and, suddenly, I actually felt a very physical weight lift from my shoulders and tears of relief consumed me. I felt lighter than I can ever remember, and I knew that a major chapter of my life had ended.

On my way back to the alteration shop, I stopped at the grocery store where my attention was pulled to the song playing on the store speaker system; *Do you believe in magic in a young girl's heart?* What a perfect ending to a perfect "story," the song/billboard that started it all. Yes, I do believe in magic/ miracles. This powerful experience taught me that there is a spiritual solution for every problem and *It is all about Me*—the small *me* finding the spiritual *Me* and thus finding life's true purpose.

Waking-Dreams That Finally Led me to the "Perfect Relationship"

I met Dave shortly after my divorce—he had just moved to town. A year later when he asked me to marry him, I knew I loved him deeply but was very reluctant to move too quickly into another marriage. I explained that I would answer when I could get past my fears. I then asked Divine Spirit for a clear sign and confirmation when to take the next step in this relationship.

A couple of months later, in January, I got the strong nudge to go to a certain store and shop for a birthday gift for my niece. At the store I couldn't find anything that felt right and pondered why I was there. As I was leaving the store, I passed the valentine cards and thought of Dave. The first card that caught my attention said, "A valentine for my fiancée." I promptly put the card back and fled the store.

The words in the card kept coming to mind, which I knew was a sign but I still resisted. I finally decided to go get the card, in part, to stop these nagging thoughts. As I opened the card in the store, I noticed that above each verse, on a line by itself, was the word "FOREVER." At that moment, my attention was pulled to the song on the store music system, "When I fall in love it will be *forever*." That did it! I knew beyond a doubt that it was time to drop my fears and take the next leap of faith. I used the card to say, "Yes." Now, eleven years after saying "I do," I continue to cherish the deep love and trust we share—forever. I knew that I had found the man with the golden heart!

Blogging With God—Potent Points to Ponder

As mentioned earlier in this chapter, the following short story was the beginning and development of my spiritual writing process.

"Don't Die With Your Music Still in You"

Years ago, pondering something became an avenue of communication with my Higher Self. Pondering served to open a doorway for a new, higher perception; a deeper connection with the sacred essence of all life. The questions became the answer; the deeper the "life question," the deeper the answer or truth. As we unravel layers of "egoistic lies" about life, God, and the Universe—the truth does set us free.

My heartfelt pondering started in the 1970's when my life wasn't working—in an unhappy marriage and no place to turn. Returning to my family, which meant living their religious beliefs of intolerance and judgment, was worse than my present situation. My family's religious teaching stated that if you don't follow their teachings, God won't hear or answer your prayers, so I stopped praying. For seven years I felt confused, abandoned, and afraid.

Then out of desperation I prayed anyway. Slowly, my life and thoughts began to change. I read the Bible again with a whole new understanding.

The "non-traditional" avenues of communication started with a lucid dream where I was told, "there is more truth than what is in your Bible," and I had a vision of two Bible verses that continue to guide my life today. I learned that Divine Guidance has many vehicles—dreams, things repeated, songs, license plates, TV, billboards, etc. Did daily life really hold messages to be played like a *living code*," waiting to be deciphered?

"Don't Die with your Music Still in You" were the words from Dr. Wayne Dyer's book, *Secrets for Success and Inner Peace,* that pulled my attention—my cue to start pondering. He mentioned that you were born for a reason and part of your job is to find that reason, and listening to your intuition, will tell you what you are passionate about. A quote in his book from Kahlil Gibran felt true: *"When you are born, your work is placed in your heart."*

Your "heart music" is what makes you feel passionate, whole, and inspired; your destiny. True peace comes by playing your own special song—let it be heard. This lets the world know why you're here—do it with Passion! Some will like it and some won't, but that isn't your concern. Don't end your life in regret because you were so afraid of not being good enough, or afraid of taking a chance, that you didn't even try.

The next message came during a TV show called *Lost*. An old familiar seventies song played in the hatch—their underground apartment, but I paid little attention to the words. The next morning at 3:00 the lyrics, modified somewhat, played in my mind: "Make your own kind of music, in your own special way." I thought of Dr. Dyer's words, "Don't die with your music still in you." I looked up the song lyrics: "You gotta make your own kind of music, sing your own special song, even if nobody else sings along."

I knew years ago that my "music/passion" was in spiritual writing. I even asked for a repeated sign when it was time to write. My sign came a couple of years ago, but my "small self" told me I didn't have time and it wasn't good enough. I started anyway—it didn't have to be shared! It helped me to realize that my writings were just my perceptions, not "the gospel" for anyone. Maybe I could step into my vulnerable place to let my own "special song" be heard, even if nobody else sings along—it doesn't matter. I knew I had to get "my music" out of me.

I pondered about what I could write that would help others. My answer came from an inspirational CD. A person asked what they could do (their music) that would help others. They were told to find their own special "niche" and the Universe would draw to them (Law of Attraction) people who are in harmony with that. Don't try to change yourself, your passion, to accommodate others. A Potent Point To Ponder! (For the full version go to: www.bloggingwithgod.com.)

A Note to the Reader

We would love to hear about your experiences with Waking Dreams. See our web site (www.thelivingcode.com) for contact information.

*   *   *

Here is an experience from one of our pre-published readers:

"I am enjoying your book very much! I want to tell you about something that happened to me that I know was a direct result of reading your book.

I was at the reference desk of the library, where I work. I was thinking of my utmost desire—to dwell in the sacred space in my heart as Drunvalo Melchizedek had taught us. I asked if I was rushing myself and being too impatient to get there.

Within 5 minutes of my asking, a student came in and went to the circulation desk to get a book to help him with taking the placement exam. He was very friendly and asked if this was the best route to take. He was talking to the student worker at the circulation desk. He then came over to talk to me and chatted about the exam. He was talking about himself, but the words that struck me dealt with the fact that he wasn't going to rush things, and instead was going to take his time. I knew instantly that his words were meant for me too.

So, thank you for writing this wonderful book! It truly is of service to truth seekers!"

L.M., Wailuku, Hawaii

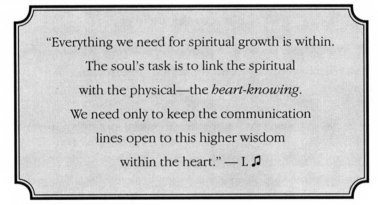

"Everything we need for spiritual growth is within.
The soul's task is to link the spiritual
with the physical—the *heart-knowing*.
We need only to keep the communication
lines open to this higher wisdom
within the heart." — L ♫

Chapter 6

WHY DOES LIFE PLAY RERUNS?

The Belief System—A Lot of B.S.

Why does life play reruns or history repeat itself?
Let's take a look!

By Linda with Brenda's ♫

In *The Power of Now* by Eckhart Tolle, he refers to the script in our mind as that aspect of our self that distorts the present moment. This aspect acts out our never-ending repeated performances of our old reactive patterns of emotions, thoughts, desires, and reactions.

Have you ever asked yourself this question, *"Why is this happening to me again?"* Perhaps you felt used again, betrayed, in financial lack again, or you just attracted the same type of personality in a relationship.

If you have noticed some painful aspect of your life that is all too familiar and it happens on a regular basis, congratulations, you are now aware of your life's reruns! You have stepped back from your life script long enough to become the Watcher—usually in disbelief—that this repeated event could have happened to you again! You may have found yourself thinking, *"How could I have been so stupid/dumb?"*

Finally, sick and tired of the endless cycle of suffering, you begin to awaken using pain and unhappiness as a catalyst for change. Though you may be frozen in fear, not knowing what to do, your actions at this point are monumental on the spiritual journey because you have finally made contact with your spiritual nature, the Watcher/Soul—an aspect that is hard-wired into the human system. The Watcher in you has observed the life events that keep you going in circles; only the faces and places have changed.

The more you practice being the Watcher, the easier it gets. This is a major step toward stopping the reruns of the script and getting out of this painful vicious cycle. It is your awakened presence as the Watcher, that breaks your identification with your painful reruns and begins to stop them from controlling your thoughts. Our painful, repeated thoughts feed energy to our unhappy life situations and keep those reruns running.

B ♫ I recall a friend, who would tell me about her problems, and very often the solution seemed to me to be "as plain as the nose on her face," but she just couldn't see it. Any suggestion from me only brought anger and defensiveness. I began to realize that her life was one trauma and drama after another—the same problems would appear but just in different wrappers; this was the rerun "disorder." Pondering her resistance to see a solution I realized that, unfortunately, the drama gave her a sense of value and attention.

She helped me learn the "art of allowing" and recognizing that others need to follow their own process of awakening—no pain, no gain. In my own life I had to reach the "bottom of the barrel" to start earnestly looking for a way out—my friend just hadn't "bottomed out" yet. The Watcher wasn't turned on and the best action for me, was *no action* or reaction—detachment.

Unfortunately, it seems that some people would rather die than change; the rerun rut is deep. These people often justify their actions by saying, "That is just the way I am!" We have our "safe and easy" routines/ruts. These ruts are so deep that they hold us captive in a hypnotic trance that we are totally unaware of. This helped me understand the "routine rut" that we all fall into, and explains our resistance to making positive changes, until life events force us to do so.

L ♫ Everything we need for spiritual growth is within. The soul's task is to link the spiritual with the physical—the *heart-knowing*. We need only to keep the communication lines open to this higher wisdom within the heart. In chapters four and five, Brenda gives examples of ways to keep these lines open. Perhaps this is why the Bible says the kingdom of heaven is within and if you seek it first, then the rest will take care of itself. Most people don't understand how to do this since the Bible is not explicit about it. The following spiritual exercise explains one way to do this.

Solving the Unsolvable Problems—a Spiritual Exercise

Once the seeking/pondering begins, this is a great formula that works unbelievably well. One way to link the spiritual with the physical (bringing heaven to earth) when faced with a seemingly unsolvable situation, especially when a rerun has been detected, is to admit, *I do not know the solution to this problem, but I know on some level there is one—how can I perceive this differently?* In doing this you are surrendering to a Higher Power. You can even add your own words at the end and affirm that all is in Divine Order, and the way will be shown to you in a timely manner.

Every time your mind, the ego, wants to chew on the issue, repeat the above sentence and let it go—authentic surrendering. Eventually, the mind gives up and, surprisingly, the perfect solution presents itself.

Usually it is one I would not have thought of, but sometimes it seems so obvious I couldn't believe I didn't see it—I had to get out of the wrong mind and into the right mind. It always seems to be a "win-win" situation for everyone involved. At times, the only action on my part is to keep surrendering to a Higher Power—*HP Solutions.*

An Angel on One shoulder and the Devil on the Other
—Who's in Charge of the Show?

In becoming aware of this Higher Power, the Watcher, we realized there are two of us sharing the same body? I have heard people say, *"I don't know what possessed me to do that."* Without knowing it, they became aware of the duality that is inherent in all of us; the angel on one shoulder and the devil on the other. When I was a child my favorite comedian, Flip Wilson, was famous for saying, *"The devil made me do it."* He always had a twinkle in his eye and a funny little grin when he said it, as if it excused him from being responsible for his actions.

Moderation in all things is a key factor to balancing this dual nature and stopping, "the devil made me do it" reruns. The Watcher is a natural stabilizer that brings balance to our angelic and devilish side—they both can get out of hand. Most of us have played the role of the self-appointed guardian angel for another, thinking we have their HP solutions, only to realize we wasted our time, energy, and often, our money.

As the Watcher, I began to understand more clearly the duality in humans the Bible calls the *worldly man* and the *spiritual man*. I always thought the worldly man was a really bad guy, a liar or a thief. Well, not so! The apostle Paul explained it very well when he said, "What I want to do, I don't, and what I don't want to do, I do."

You will find a deeper understanding of the Watcher—our spiritual nature/man and the ego/worldly man in the book *The Power of Now,* and *A New Earth* by Eckhart Tolle. He gives an in-depth view of the duality of our human nature.

Reruns—Life's Flypaper—Before You Know It You Are Trapped!

On this planet, the negative and positive live side by side, and at times, it may be difficult to tell the difference. The ego is very cunning and the trap it lays for us is like flypaper. It loves to entangle us in our sticky emotional script, imprisoning us in our old belief system; the next thing we know we feel stuck again and find ourselves saying, *"Why is this happening to me, again?"*

The Watcher is very handy to have around. Once you let your intention be known, that you want to see more of the Watcher, it will introduce you to some new friends: *Detachment* and *Discernment*. With Discernment, which is often the silent pause before you speak, it is easier to avoid being trapped in the flypaper and with Detachment you will find good seats on the sidelines of the script. From this seat, there certainly is less wear and tear on the body— less stress, not to mention more peace of mind. A good Biblical description is *be in the world, and not of the world.*

My definition of detachment does not mean unemotional or uncaring. We will all have a certain amount of pain and pleasure in our life experiences. If we get knocked down, we just get up, dust ourselves off, and go again. Understanding that the purpose of those traumatic events is for spiritual growth will keep you from being stuck on the emotional flypaper for the rest of your life.

Detachment and discernment will help you keep the emotions in balance. One of our great lessons today is learning discernment. There is a wealth of information on the Internet and bookshelves but we have to discern what is true for us. If the correct information is important, your IGS will direct you to the answer for you. Remember, it may not be truth for your neighbor, so be very cautious about insisting that if it worked for you, it must work for everyone. Practice the *art of allowing*.

Who's driving your car?

After you switch back and forth between the ego and the Watcher, it will become more obvious who's in the driver's seat. You finally realize how much more comfortable it is to cruise along with the Watcher than experience the roller coaster ride of the ego. Then, you will do your best to stay awake in the present moment while you navigate through life.

ASK: How Can I Perceive This Differently?

If you do happen to get caught in the emotional flypaper, a quick way to put the Watcher back in the driver's seat is to ask, "How can I perceive this differently?" Or as *The 50 Miracle Principles* of *A Course in Miracles* by Kenneth Wapnick states, "*The course says the only thing we should ever ask of anything in this world is: What is it for? What purpose does it serve?*"

Asking these questions keeps you out of the ego-habit of criticizing/ judging and puts your focus on the HP solution, and thus, keeping the spiritual communication lines open. This begins our true healing of the ego's perception that we are separate from God.

A Course in Miracles teaches the same thing but with different terminology; there are only two purposes in the world: the ego's purpose or the Holy Spirit's purpose.

The Course, as stated in *The 50 Miracles Principles*, also teaches that the function of the Holy Spirit and Jesus are synonymous; "both serve the function of being the internal Teacher or the inner Voice that will lead us home." Jesus was the first to transcend His dual nature, thus, making the Holy Spirit the only voice within—*the Father and I are one.* This explains His words—*what I do you can do, and more.* In this book we have chosen to use the terms Watcher/Soul/Intuition, in most cases, instead of Jesus and Holy Spirit. They all function as the internal teacher or inner voice.

B ♫ I have used the above questions countless times, with amazing results. It seems to be the vital key that activates our intuitive nature—the truth center. I have suggested this to clients many times.

One client had a lot of self-anger that was expressing outwardly in his life experiences. Finally, I helped him understand that the outer life is a reflection of the inner thoughts and attitudes. I asked him to start repeating this question until he had an answer: "How can I perceive this differently?"

The next time we met, I was so proud of his efforts because for the first time since we began working together, he had taken responsibility for creating his life situations. He now understood that his chronic health issues, and subsequent unfair situations, served the purpose of helping him to learn to recognize, and heal, the self-anger that was hindering his spiritual growth. This was a huge revelation, helping him move out of the resistance of "what is" and into a state of acceptance and allowing. This act of surrendering put him back in the driver's seat.

Self-Knowledge Learned Through Numerology

L ♫ As I mentioned earlier in one of my stories, Spirit guided me to the library to find answers to life's questions—what a great place to shop for new ideas. Since I had many questions, I became a frequent shopper—Why *does* life play reruns?

With each book that I carried home to ponder, Spirit would send me an experience in life related to the information in the book. The experience caused the new idea to become a part of my *self-knowledge*, thus, updating my old belief system. This changed my beliefs from theoretical to experiential—something no one could take from me. Through this process I was learning to renew my mind daily.

One day, while searching the library shelves, I came across a book on numerology—*Numerology and The Divine Triangle*. This was another turning point in my life. Only a few months prior to this, I would never have entertained the thought of reading a book about numbers—I would have considered it taboo.

In a short time I was learning an incredible amount of information about myself: the good, the bad, and the potential. Surprisingly, these new insights were very accurate. My internal book of self-knowledge was expanding rapidly. As mentioned in the previous chapter, numbers became one of our favorite avenues for IGS communications.

Since our focus was on following Spirit, we were never tempted to make numerology our god, and thus not step out of our house unless we had consulted our numbers for the day. For us, numerology was only a step on our path back home to God. We knew not to get sidetracked on our journey.

Why DOES Life Play Reruns?

After I began studying numerology, it took me over a year to connect an important piece of the puzzle regarding, *why life plays reruns.* As I studied how the numbers worked, *Numerology and The Divine Triangle* taught me how to calculate the numbers that would influence my new personal year and month. Even when I would forget to check my numbers, I was in awe of how accurate the information had been after the fact. I would make little notes in my book on some of the more significant events of that month.

It would take a year for my personal monthly numbers to cycle around again, and the results amazed me. I would compare notes for my monthly number with the previous year, and I discovered that my life was going in circles—reruns. To my amazement, I experienced the same situations over and over again each year, but they were wearing different faces and happening in new places. The numbers rotated one number each month as I spiraled up the number scale, reaching a new, higher number, for the first month, at the beginning of each birth year.

A good example of this is the Personal Numbers we were in at the time of writing this book, based on the book, *Numerology and the Divine Triangle*. We gave birth to the idea of co-authoring a book just at the end of our 33/6 Personal Year—33 is a master number, resonating with the highest level of love and compassion. This means we wrote a good part of the book under the following Personal Year, which was 34/7—this number has to do with completion, achievement, self-analysis, and is connected with the hidden mysteries of life. We finished the manuscript in a 35/8 year—preparedness, recognition, business, responsibility—whatever the job is, get it done. The final edit and publication was in a 36/9 year—"...persevere with relentless determination. Remain intent upon your goal and have confidence that it will soon be reached...have joy in the prospect of this completion." We did not sit down with the numerology book to plan this. When you are *tuned in and turned on* to Spirit's guidance life events will then be in a natural flow.

"Recognize the threshold between what is really new and what is a repetition of old patterns under a new guise." — Trigueirinho

It became obvious, as I watched the cycles in my life through the numbers, that history did repeat itself with profound similarities! This greatly explained the reruns happening over and over again, but on a broader scale. Once I became aware of this, I began journaling my experiences in the different Personal Number months and worked with changing my reactions to the repeated cycles—especially the ones that were character flaws, such as jealousy in relationships.

Since I had a preview of what could possibly happen, I could be more alert and on the watch for it. It was amazing that with just a little knowledge about myself—self-knowledge—I could make course corrections in my actions and emotional reactions. Sometimes I won, sometimes I lost, but by now all that mattered was that I played the game consciously aware of what was happening.

Ponderism: *A broader picture: If we have individual rhythms, would it not stand to reason that perhaps each nation has a rhythm—perhaps Humanity itself has a collective rhythm? A rhythm within a rhythm—perhaps we are talking about something like a radio band with different frequencies comprising the whole band. Perhaps ancient prophecies are warnings; if we don't change the rhythm, this is the end result.*

History does not have to repeat itself. If we become the Watcher and make conscious efforts to change the negative rerun patterns that we observe within, and by choosing a different response, then our past can become a great teacher.

To help the brain accept this more easily, try doing things the opposite of what you would normally do them, such as brushing your teeth with the opposite hand. When I told Brenda this, I got an e-mail back saying she decided to try this by putting on her pants with the left leg first. Early in the morning, by the light of the moon, she ended up with the left leg in the right leg of the pants and decided this might not be as easy as it sounds. But she had a good laugh and knew I would enjoy the story.

The prophecies for today's time hold warnings for our world of what will happen if we keep going in the same old circles—playing the collective reruns—and if we don't change the old habit patterns. Always remember, *a prophecy is not set in stone—a good prophecy is a failed prophecy.* Developing contact with our Intuitive Guidance System—living from the "heart-knowing"—will put us in the right place at the right time.

A Little Self-Knowledge Goes a Long Way in Changing Our Reruns

In the mid-nineties Brenda came to live with me. We were both single again at age forty-four. In some ways we picked up right where we left off in high school; the boys (now men) always seemed to like her more than me. In high school she had a steady boyfriend and I didn't; thus, I had more time to study but made only slightly higher grades. She equated this to meaning that I was smarter than she and this kept her in the reruns of *not good enough.* This, of course, brought up jealousy and competition issues for both of us. Brenda now realizes that no matter how much she studied in high school, her fear of not being good enough caused her to mentally freeze up during a test.

Like everyone, we had our challenges growing up. But now, having studied our numbers, we both came to an understanding about our rerun patterns. In her numbers, Brenda had some issues to heal involving the opposite sex, so this explained to me why the boys were more interested in her than me. I have come to greatly appreciate the work she came into this life to do in this area, and I am so grateful I did not have that challenge. After all, I was given my own lessons to work on—jealousy in relationships.

When Brenda came to live with me, I owned a successful alteration shop. I am thankful that we had learned to sew at an early age and had quickly become master seamstresses. Wanting to heal from a traumatic relationship, Brenda turned in her corporate desk for a sewing machine.

She came at a time when I really needed her help and we enjoyed working together. I decided it was a great opportunity to put to use the tools the Holy Spirit had given me over the years and to change this rerun pattern of jealousy in the dating game.

By this time, we both were well aware of repeated patterns, and were now able to discussed the situations freely. With Brenda's encouragement, I began to focus on my own beauty instead of comparing myself to her when we were around men. I began to feel better about myself and my looks. Focusing on my good traits, without comparing, seemed to minimize how I felt about my short-comings as my inner beauty began to shine.

Around this time we "just happened" to be flying to a weekend spiritual seminar. We walked into a large auditorium that was filled with people, so I asked, inwardly, for the best place for us to sit. I ended up next to a nice gentleman and we struck up a conversation. He was a pilot and quite good looking. We saw each other several times during the seminar.

As Brenda and I discussed this later, I realized his focus was totally on me —he never gave her a second glance, which was totally out of the ordinary pattern we were used to. I felt the shift within me, which encouraged me to continue my quest for freedom from my jealousy pattern.

Little did I know that it would take me years of intense work to finally be free of this painful pattern. At the time, it seemed like it was a never ending job, but to keep it in perspective, I had to wonder how many lifetimes I had been working on this one. The end result was the peace of mind I obtained, and it was worth all the painful experiences.

I will share my first experience of becoming the Watcher and how I used the information given to me to break out of a self-imposed prison cell that I didn't even know I was in. I would not find out for many years how significant this experience was for me on a spiritual level.

Ponderism: *If we don't want the ego in the driver's seat, how do we change drivers?*

Linda's First Experience with the Watcher!
—How to Break the Habitual Cycles of Life

I had not realized how sensitive I was in taking life events too personally, until after I married at the early age of nineteen. The first year of marriage seemed to show me a lot about myself that I did not know, mostly from the voice of my husband. Within a few months of the marriage, my husband told me that he did not like the way my personality changed when we went for our weekly visit with my family—I was devastated. At the time, I was in the role of trying to "please and obey your husband," as our church doctrine taught. My "people-pleasing personality" was being criticized and I really didn't understand just what he was talking about, so I denied it.

My husband did me a great service. He forced the Watcher, in me, to come out of hiding. To my disbelief, as I observed myself, I discovered he was right. This was my first introduction to "the Watcher." What I saw amazed me. It was too obvious to ignore and, of course, being new to the family, he was the only one that could observe my change in personality. I was thankful that, instead of being upset and going into denial with this self-discovery, I became intrigued by it.

You Can't Escape Until You Have KNOWLEDGE of Your Captivity

I began to observe the personality shift that would appear the minute I put my foot in the door for the weekly family visit. With this knowledge, I began pondering my escape route.

Even though my husband never brought up the subject again, the fire was lit and I decided this aspect of myself had to go. I soon found how ingrained repeated patterns were in my belief system and how hard it is to break habits. At first, I would find myself halfway through my weekly visit before I realized I was captured again.

There were plenty of opportunities that first year of marriage to awaken to my captivity and plan my escape. I began to treat my escape much like a game plan; this kept me out of self-judgment. With each visit, I would try to wake up sooner and sooner and stop the role playing. I even patted myself on the back if I woke up shortly after I arrived. No one in the family seemed to notice since the changes were stretched out over a period of time.

Finally, I made it! Even before I entered the door, the Watcher was on guard and I walked out of prison. Yippee! I had escaped captivity from none other than my own ego-based belief system. From that moment on, I could easily identify the roles that I, and others, were playing, in a non-judgmental way. Because of this, I often made excuses for people, giving them the benefit of the doubt, because I knew that they, too, were held captive and just needed a wake-up call like I had.

Coincidently, soon after I walked out of this *prison of my mind*, we moved far enough away that I could only visit my family a few times a year. This is also a characteristic of the path. When you have learned the lesson, it is time to move on to the next one. People, places, or things can come into or leave your life at any time when a lesson has been learned—a good detachment lesson!

Life is not About Lessons, but Choices
—From the Choices Come the Lessons

It has been said that life is about learning lessons. I would like to take this phrase to the next level by saying that *life is not so much about learning lessons as it is about making choices* at life's crossroad moments, and from those choices come the lessons. In the world today, unless we become the Watcher, making our choices from our higher selves, our choices are made automatically by the default system—our subconscious belief system. This is why we are told to *know thyself*; know your human and divine tendencies. Our lessons will change when we learn to discern who is making the choices that affect our life situations.

Observing others' experiences, can often help you find what is in your belief system and make a course correction without having to experience similar pain. A former co-worker of mine exemplified how the belief system takes over when we are in certain repeated circumstances.

I began to notice that my co-worker would change her voice and mannerisms when she talked to our boss, whether it was on the phone or in person. After she said, "Hello," I could tell when he was the caller just by the way she changed her mannerisms. When she would hear his voice on the phone, she transformed into an indecisive, rattled person with low self-confidence. This was totally different from the decisive, confident person of only a few seconds before. I was fascinated by this sudden shift in her and pondered why this happened!

The answer was revealed in her own spoken words when I noticed that each time she hung up the phone from his calls she would say, "I know he thinks I am a clumsy fool, after the way I blubber my words. He's always in a hurry and I can't think fast enough for him." It never occurred to her that she had the power to change this script.

This brought understanding to the phrase, "life is a self-fulfilling prophecy." We literally prophesy some of what is going to happen to us just by the words that come out of our mouth, on a repeated basis. We will cover this in the next chapter on clichés.

The Bible says, *"As a man thinks in his heart, so is he."* My co-worker thought she was a blubbering fool when confronted by our boss. The sad part was that, in her heart, she believed it and so it was!

We establish our belief system through our thinking, because a belief is just a thought that we keep thinking over and over again. The more emotion we carry with a thought, the quicker it is deposited into our subconscious mind as part of our truth/beliefs. What we are, do, and, what is happening to us in life is the direct reflection of our belief systems. This confirmed for me my conclusions about my co-worker and her *Belief System*. By now you may realize that I have little use for our unconscious *B.S.* as I watch it sabotage peoples' lives.

Ponderism: *How much of the past defines who we are today? Do you suppose that my co-worker really believed her boss thought her to be a clumsy fool? Did her beliefs about herself have anything to do with the sudden personality change I saw?*

Yes, if we establish our belief systems with our thoughts. She prophesied what the boss thought of her and reinforced it each time she was confronted by him. She was captured by her beliefs and didn't know it. Once the Watcher comes on board, you will recognize the captive events as you play them out. It is a funny feeling to be both the observer and the participant. You certainly feel the duality mentioned earlier. Our belief systems can be our worst enemies or our best friends, depending on whether we are caught in the circles of life or reaching for a higher level.

Ponderism: *Is there a connection between why my life plays reruns and what people call karma? Do ALL actions have consequences?*

The Law of Karma

The Law of Karma is very simple and can be put into a few words: *Whatsoever a man soweth, that shall he also reap.*

The human consciousness has a blind spot when it comes to this cause-and-effect law; all actions, including thoughts, have consequences. In the last few years, the word karma has become a buzz word. I have even listened in amazement to my friends in traditional religion using it. The Law of Karma is under an even greater law, the Law of Equilibrium, which is the Law of Balance meaning that for every action there is a reaction. The prophecies we spoke of earlier are all based on the Law of Equilibrium; stay in balance or reap the consequences.

The Law of Balance reminds me of the Golden Rule I was taught as a child; *do unto others as you would have them do unto you.* This law hounded me when I was a child. If I crossed the golden line too far, I paid for it. Our brothers played endless jokes on us but when I tried to reciprocate, it always backfired. Obviously, the Golden Rule was ingrained in my belief system. My family always thought I was the golden girl, as Brenda will attest. Little did they know that I walked a tight rope even as a child.

In essence, the Golden Rule puts life on a very simple level. If you don't like being lied to, then don't lie to others, because it keeps you on the perpetual karmic wheel. *The Golden Rule is designed to help you dissolve karmic debt, if you will just follow it.*

The Bible teaches moderation in all things, and even the Buddha came to realize the importance of the "middle way" on his spiritual journey—the Law of Balance. He started life as a rich young man, protected from seeing poverty or sorrow. He wanted to experience the opposite, so he gave up his riches and even begged for food. After experiencing many of life's opposites, he eventually came to the conclusion that there must be some way to live a life that is well-balanced. He then sought the middle way. The Law of Moderation in all things has its merits, as the Buddha taught.

Is God Responsible for Our Karma—Good or Bad?

B ♫ Years ago, I was prompted to ponder the scripture—*As a man thinketh in his heart, so is he—Proverbs 23:7.* At that time, a lady called me on the phone wanting answers about why her life always seemed to be in turmoil. She was raised a Christian and wanted to blame God for all her problems. She felt that God had abandoned her because He *allowed* all these terrible things to happen to her.

I stopped her in mid-sentence; I was tired of people using God as a scapegoat for their misery and mentioned the above Bible verse. I explained that what you think in your heart is what you dwell on the most, and through the Law of Attraction, what you draw into your life.

God, in this context, is out of the picture because you have free will to choose your thoughts and choices. I also explained that she had to take responsibility for her own life and happiness and that God didn't do anything to her—she did it all to herself!

Ponderism: *Can we really balance our karmic debt in this lifetime?*

L ♫ Understanding the Law of Karma brought great relief to me. I came to understand that events in my life were a result of interactions between cause and effect rather than a punishing God, the devil, or mere chance. Because of the Law of Equilibrium, we can restore balance to negative karmic debt. The workbook for *A Course In Miracles (ACIM)* is a great teacher on how to avoid conflict, which creates more negative karma. Gary Renard, in his book, *Disappearance of the Universe* tells how *ACIM* impacted his life when he first began to study it. Through his actions of stopping conflict in his life, he began to balance his karmic debt instead of incurring more. With this understanding of true forgiveness, he began the journey in breaking the karmic bonds.

Do We Really Affect the World Around Us?

Picture this: a pebble thrown into a pond. The ripples spread out in ever-widening circles, affecting everything in their path in varying degrees and intensity. Take this analogy and apply it to everything you do on the mental, emotional, and physical levels. Every thought, every emotion, every physical action creates a vibration that has a rippling effect in the Universe. Our mental and emotional actions have a stronger effect than physical actions because our emotional thoughts hold more energy, i.e., you always know when someone is angry!

To my understanding, each ripple we make, in time, is recorded by the record keeper; in the Bible this record is referred to as the Book of Life, others refer to it as the Akashic Records. It keeps records of both good and bad karma, which are a result of our thoughts, actions, and reactions. It is this record that keeps the karmic wheels turning in the script of life, unless we wake up and choose to opt out.

Planet Earth has become a school house for many of us wanting to detach from the karmic flypaper. Balancing our karmic debts appears to be one of our purposes for being here.

Many masters have come to teach us how to do this, Jesus and the

Buddha were among them. When Jesus said, *as I am lifted up so are you*, He was not talking about His divinity but a vibrational law—resonance and entrainment. We are all energetically connected in a sea of energy. When one of us raises our vibration by changing the reactive patterns of our personality-ego, it makes it easier for others to follow suit. The flypaper just became less sticky for everyone. It's like one fly learning the secret of how to get off the flypaper, then passing it on to others—the hundredth monkey effect. Eventually, we learn from others' experiences and no one gets on the flypaper—we know better!

Master Jesus, *the way shower,* came to tell us that the Law of Love is a higher law than the Law of Karma. His teachings were about learning to live these new laws that He came to implement on the planet. St. Augustine also said, *"Love and do what you will."* In other words, with love in your heart, everything you do will be an extension of that love.

We can't take any of our karmic baggage with us into these higher frequencies. All debts have to be paid-in-full on all levels as a person, a nation, and a planet. On some level people are feeling this. There seems to be a new wave of energy in the United States to get out of debt and stop the credit card spending addiction, not to mention taking better care of ourselves on all levels, and taking better care of our planet.

The Law of Karma is No Respecter of Persons

Every word and action is a fingerprint of your electronic signature, and when the Book of Life, as mentioned in the Christian Bible is reviewed there is no chance of a computer error—the effects of a thought or an action are returned to its sender. The law is *no respecter of persons*; in fact, its job is to simply return what was sent out—no more, no less—end of story! This is called karmic return and is what the world is experiencing now.

What keeps people from connecting the dots of their thoughts and actions with what they are receiving in life is the delayed reaction. This delayed reaction is done for our benefit, so that we are not hit with a "blast from the past" that knocks us off the planet before we even have a chance to balance our stuff—karma. This is the reason for reincarnation.

Ponderism: *Can we go beyond Karma?*

This was a major pondering question when I began to consciously balance my karma. In his book, *Beyond Karma*, Trigueirinho sums it up beautifully.

"In these times, more and more people are finding the strength to deal with the effects of their past actions and are on the way to transcending the law of karma. They do so mainly by being dedicated to a supreme and divine power and by facing life situations dispassionately. They are able to put aside the notion that fulfilling an obligation is burdensome. The ones who naturally express the energy of love regard their duties as tasks to be fulfilled because these contribute to the greater good. They do everything with simplicity, without complaining or commenting or engaging in superfluous reasoning—a benign way of moving beyond the sphere of the law of karma... Human karma is mainly part of the ego. Therefore, to be able to transcend the sphere of the law of cause and effect, one's soul or a higher nucleus of consciousness must govern one's existence."

Exercise to Stop the Rerun Rut—Connect With the HP Solution

I am finding people who have not totally grasped Eckhart Tolle's comments about staying in the NOW, as mentioned in his book *The Power of Now*. He explains that being present in each moment means that you take each life situation as it comes to you and use it for spiritual growth. In no way do you skirt around a problem and ignore it, thinking this is what it means to stay in the present moment. If you find your present moment intolerable, Tolle gives three options for an *HP solution*. You can remove yourself from the situation, change it, or accept it.

Surrender to what life has presented you. If you can't afford a new house, learn to accept the old one—maybe remodel it. We have experienced that once we let go of our perception of the situation, it shifts. The only real solution to any problem is to solve our inner conflict with it—resistance. Make peace where you are by leaving the situation, modifying it, or move into allowing, "what is, is," especially, if the circumstances are out of your control.

I used to be annoyed at my husband for squeezing the toothpaste in the middle of the tube each time. I realized the inner turmoil I had created over such an insignificant thing and pondered what the solution might be. Getting my own tube of toothpaste solved the problem beautifully...Duh!

Life really can be simplified if we just pay attention. I then enjoyed watching just how mangled that tube would get before he decided to change the habit and squeeze elsewhere. I decided not to get "bent out of shape," but instead pondered how to regain my "inner peace."

In the next chapter we will explore how many of our reruns are created by our habitual clichés—life IS a self-fulfilling prophecy—unless we consciously change the Rerun Ruts.

Chapter 7

CLICHÉS THAT HOLD US CAPTIVE

Change Your Clichés—Change Your Life

"Habitual thought, and not environment or circumstances, has made you what you are."
— Wallace D. Wattles

"Not that which goeth into the mouth defileth a man; but that which cometh out of the mouth, this defileth a man...But those things which proceed out of the mouth come forth from the heart; and they defile the man."
— Matthew 15:11, 18 KJV

By Linda with Brenda's ♫

Many personal problems can be traced to the words that come out of our mouths, especially our clichés. These are trite phrases repeated flippantly, such as, "that blows my mind" or "let me pick your brain." Ancient wisdom, in the quote above, is quite clear; our thoughts are what hurts us rather than our food. I have pondered whether or not we are drawn to food with certain vibrations because of our vibrational thoughts, thus, harmful thoughts equal harmful food.

In this chapter we will explain, briefly, how clichés can harm or help us. The key is to be more conscious of what we repeatedly say and think, if we want to create positive changes in our life situations.

B ♪ In his book, *Your Thoughts Can Change Your Life*, Donald Curtis, uses the analogy of a movie projector and film in relating to our daily life, to help us understand the importance of the spoken word. Curtis points out that our life is a projection, an image of all of our thoughts, feelings, actions and spoken words. The film is our true nature but can become out of focus and distorted by our conditioned perceptions of life experiences. In other words, the script running in our "life movie" is a result of everything we feel, think, do, and say. If any part of your life looks like a trauma and drama soap opera, you are the only one who can change it; start by changing or stopping your habitual clichés and watch your life change for the better.

If you really want to turn your life situations around quickly, just let the Watcher alert you to some of the clichés that you are saying or thinking out of habit—then stop saying them.

L ♪ *Cliché Exercise:* For several days collect clichés that you hear yourself and others saying. Then ask yourself this question, "What if that cliché were taken literally, would I continue to say it?"

Ponderism: *Could it be that our clichés keep our life going in circles?*

How often do we pay attention to the ingrained childhood clichés from our parents and ponder the part they play in shaping our lives? It shouldn't be any surprise when we get older that we become more and more like our parents, *if we are still thinking their thoughts!* What about those painful words spoken to us (perhaps by our parents or childhood peers) that we keep repeating in our heads, and, thus, they unconsciously control our life situations? These experiences often left us with low self-esteem—feeling stupid, dumb, or not good enough. Are we passing these on to our children?

Change Your Clichés and Change Your Life

I would like to share the story of a co-worker who was held captive for five weeks because of her habitual clichés. She created a little longer vacation from work than she had intended.

One morning, my co-worker called me at home to say she had broken her wrist. She said that she would be off work for four or five weeks and needed me to take her place managing the store. I said, "You got the break you wanted." She was always saying, "Give me a break!" She got my message and replied that she needed a break, but not like this.

She didn't understand the principle of how her thoughts affected her life—you reap what you "say." Ignorance is not bliss and can even turn into superstition if we don't understand this basic truth. Someone probably passed under a ladder and got hurt; thus, it became a symbol of bad luck to walk under a ladder. The really sad and unnerving part is that if you believe these trite sayings to be true, then you need to honor that belief because you drastically increase the odds of it happening—this is the Law of Attraction.

This event with my co-worker was a part of my lesson on the importance of the spoken word and being careful of what you say, as you might just get it. When something is repeated often enough, it goes into the subconscious belief system as *our truth*. This is how hypnosis works; repetition and rhythm. The subconscious then acts as a magnet, delivering to you what it is you continually think about. Like a computer, it does not have the capability to discern if this is good or bad for you, it just knows what your repeated focus is—your prayer.

Ponderism: *Is every thought like a prayer waiting to be answered?* (The more emotional feeling put into the prayer-thoughts, the faster the return in the material world.)

Both of us, can personally testify to having the experience of financial lack. Our finances turned around when we learned what was in our belief system that held us financially captive. We learned to make conscious choices that ended the old, childhood thought patterns of lack—there's never enough.

Spirit gave me the following abundance lesson. When my husband mentioned that I needed a new car, I found myself thinking and saying, "We can't afford one." I had not bought a brand-new car in thirty years, and I assured him the high monthly payments on a new car would not fit into our present budget. After two weeks of thinking, "I can't afford one," I realized I was living the consequences of those thoughts and made a conscious effort to say the opposite when the negative thought came up—"I *can* afford a new car." Within two days, a previous boss called to ask if I would work one day a week. When I did the math, I would not only earn enough for my monthly car payment but it covered insurance also—an abundance lesson I will never forget. I have stopped thinking and saying "I can't afford that."

Abundance Phrase to Counter Clichés of Lack

We both noticed a change in our spending habits when we started changing our clichés of lack; the desire to buy (have-to-have) things was drastically reduced—taking us out of the consumerism addiction. We started noticing and appreciating the abundance that we already had, such as a closet full of clothes; now *all of our needs are easily and effortlessly met—with plenty to spare and plenty to share.* I repeat this cliché each time I give something to someone, thus reinforcing it.

I was at a really low point financially when I came up with this concept in order to stop my anxious mind, "If my investments paid out tomorrow, would I worry about the bills today?" I would make myself stop and *feel the relief* of that happening. I could feel such a huge shift in my energy field as I did this. Each time my mind wanted to worry about the bills, I would stop and repeat the above phrase and feel the relief. It began to work as explained in the next paragraph. Being anxious for nothing, as the Bible says, was beginning to pay off. This was truly the beginning-of-the-end of *lack* consciousness for me.

One of the clichés I used when it was really tough to pay the bills was, "I always have money left at the end of the month after paying my bills." Interesting events began to happen that would give us extra cash, such as our air conditioner on our rented house needed repair, so we paid the bill with a credit card and deducted the amount off of our rent. This extra cash flow in the bank gave me just enough to pay the bills that month. My thought was, WOW something is working! Within a few months we moved and our finances began to change and we found ourselves making such statements as, "I always pay cash for my purchases." Life situations stopped grabbing my money like they used to.

At the same time, unknown to me, Brenda would say with strong feeling, "I always have an extra hundred dollars at the end of the month after paying my bills." She would increase the amount in increments as the goal manifested, even to the point of eventually maintaining a balance of two thousand dollars in her bank account at the end of the month.

Brenda and I had gone through *A Course in Miracles* workbook and the following year, on our birthday, we began studying *The 50 Miracle Principles of A Course in Miracles* book—one principle each week. Principle 41 gave us an idea for a counter-phrase for any thoughts of lack.

> *"Wholeness is the perceptual content of miracles. They thus correct...
> the faulty perception of lack."*

Some thoughts are very subtle, so let the Watcher do what it does best and help you uncover those tricky *slight of the mind* thoughts. With any feeling of lack we would say to Spirit, "Heal my misperception of lack."

When we read Principle 41 it became very clear that lack was only a perception of the mind. This helped us to start focusing on abundance rather than lack in our lives.

I even went through my kitchen and decided if I had two of anything, I had abundance. If I felt lack, such as needing more measuring cups (an inexpensive item), I would go buy them in order to feel abundant. Doing this with the little things soon carried over to the big things. I started balancing my check book differently. I rounded off the dollar amounts to an even number, thus, dropping the concept of "pinching pennies." By the end of the month, I had always gained a few dollars in my bank account.

B ♫ In the late 1990's, a student in one of my classes gave me a most profound clue regarding finances—one that brought a continued awareness of my own financial clichés. The subject of financial lack came up during the class and the student explained that she has *never had a thought that the finances wouldn't be there*—her core belief.

I was amazed at this concept knowing that, most likely, I had never had a thought, on a consistent basis, that the finances *would be* there—this was such a foreign concept. I knew after the student's comment that I had to make a committed effort to changing my financial clichés. My Watcher began to tag my unconscious lack clichés which, in itself, was a process to dissolve them.

I also noticed that building my self-esteem and honoring my inner nudges had a direct connection to financial abundance. Abundance had little to do with outer circumstances—it was totally an inside job.

Our childhood reflected that financial lack and worry about money was just a way of life. We certainly had a lot of mental house cleaning to do in this area—*you have to work hard to make ends meet*—well that's just a bunch of baloney as we would say down on the farm.

For more information on these concepts, *Open Your Mind to Prosperity* by Catherine Ponder is an excellent book to read.

L ♫ Read the list below to give your Watcher a jump start on this great transforming process. Check the ones you have heard yourself or others say.

Clichés

That just makes me sick to my stomach

Everything falls apart after fifty

That disease runs in my family

No pain no gain

That just blows my mind

I should have my head examined

I need this like I need a whole in my head

I am out of my mind with...worry, fear, grief

Give me a break

My feet are killing me

I can't stand that

Let me pick your brain

You are a glutton for punishment

I nearly died when he/she said/did

You have to work hard to make a living

You/I just can't win

You don't deserve it

This always happens to me

Down to the last dime

There's never enough

Pinching every penny—nothing comes easy

Living hand to mouth

I can't get anything right

We can't afford that

Easy come easy go

That's just my luck

I'll never be good enough

That: was a pain in the neck

...breaks my heart

...drives me crazy

...will give me a heart attack

...will be the death of me

...just kills me

Life is just one thing after another

I'm always in the way

What's the use, it won't work anyway

_____ always happens to me

Can't make ends meet

Positive clichés to reprogram your belief system (B.S.)

Note: Be sure to imagine and feel as if these desires were already fulfilled. The more you focus on these, the quicker they will manifest. Your clichés, said with conviction, will pull to you the very things required to fulfill them—it's a Universal law of attraction—it has to happen! Caution, be careful for what you ask; you might just get it!

- Money always comes easily and effortlessly
- I always have $ _____ left in the bank after all bills are paid
- I always have plenty to spare and plenty to share
- I always work less and make more
- I always have plenty of money in my wallet
- I always pay cash for everything
- Everything I need comes to me easily and effortlessly
- My timing is always just right
- I always have more than enough
- I always experience vibrant health and well being
- My immune systems is always radiantly healthy and strong
- Every cell, system and organ has vitality and strength
- Be specific with any goal: My blood pressure is always normal
- I love the source that I am

Make up your own clichés and reinforce them until you observe changes in your life. For additional clichés, we recommend the following books: *Your Body Believes Every Word You Say* by Barbara Hoberman Levine and *Your Thoughts Can Change your Life* by Donald Curtis.

Perhaps some of the clichés of childhood no longer fit, but have we done any housecleaning to clean out the cobwebs of the past? "Don't talk to strangers" is perhaps good for a child, but there were no rules as to what age you can begin to talk to strangers. As an adult, this could bring loneliness and isolation, especially if you are an introvert. Some other childhood clichés directed at boys are; "Act like a man" or "Boys don't cry?" Is it possible that this is an underlying current to why men often hide their feelings?

Create Your Own Clichés

We both have realized the value in self-created clichés to reinforce the positive events in our lives. The following stories are a good example of our experiences with this concept.

L ♫ I have always had good luck while traveling. I lived in Denver for a while and my self-created cliché of believing, *"I always have good luck getting on a busy freeway,"* helped me, many times, to handle rush hour traffic. I would give gratitude each time I entered the freeway and reinforced it by repeating my cliché.

B ♫ I look at my fear and then make up an affirmation or cliché that will counteract it. When we moved to a new home and the route to my job changed, I had to rethink the traffic situation. The shortest route involved a left-hand turn requiring me to pull out across traffic, which always left me feeling anxious about having an accident. I knew I needed to change these feelings/thoughts because I would eventually be creating this as a reality. I began to affirm daily, "When driving on this street I am always safe." This opened me to new possibilities and, in a few days, I received a strong inner nudge to go a different route, which was much safer and faster, to my surprise. My new route now reflected my new clichés.

After my divorce I needed to make several road trips and each one would be eleven hours long each way. Thankfully, with Divine help, I had a new car but I was still a little anxious about this long drive by myself. I decided to start a helpful cliché: "My automobile always gets me home." I would repeat this often and feel grateful that it would be done. I knew this repetition combined with emotional feeling, would get it into my belief system.

On one trip I was still about one hundred miles from home and noticed at a stop for gas that it took a couple of tries to get my car started, which never happens. I pulled into my drive way at home and turned off the engine and decided to just check it again. The car wouldn't start. As it turned out I needed a new battery, but my cliché worked as my car always got me home!

How Many of Our Heart Thoughts Define Who We Are Today?

"As a man thinketh in his heart so is he." Proverbs 23:7

L ♫   As I mentioned before, our belief systems contain what we "are taught" or "is caught" by the age of six—our childhood programming.

I can remember my first husband, who was a minister, always saying, "That's just the way I am." This is what he believed to be true about himself and was his excuse not to change.

I remember him telling me that he grew up on the streets in a large city, and in school his older brothers had a bad reputation for being trouble-makers. He related this story of being a freshman in high school: In his first gym class, the coach picked him up by the shirt and pinned him against the wall saying, "If you are like your brothers, I don't want any trouble." He was very embarrassed.

Is it any wonder he didn't feel good about himself? He was very different than his brothers and grew up wanting to be a priest but, there again, didn't feel good enough. This guilt carried over into his life as a preacher. Only after our divorce and my study of self-help books, did I begin to realize the impact his childhood had on his adult life.

He died of AIDS within a few days of his fiftieth birthday. "Nobody cares," and "I am not good enough," are two of the clichés that an AIDS person has in their heart-thoughts, as explained by Louise Hay, in her book; *You Can Heal Your Life*.

I had sent him my personal copy of her book a few months before he died, not knowing he was terminally ill. I found it in the personal items that he brought to the hospital a week before my children (now young adults) and I were called to his death bed. We had not seen him in several years, and were surprised to find that none of his family came to the hospital to see him before he died. After studying the clichés for AIDS, I understood why.

He had not been a father to our children since our divorce many years prior, but we were all able to receive closure with this relationship. With much compassion, our daughters were finally able to tell him they loved him. The compassion I felt was overwhelming. I knew his problems came from his unconscious belief system and the guilt he was unable to overcome. Just like he had helped me to bring the Watcher into my life, when we first married, in his death, he taught me to embody a compassion that I had never felt before.

Had the girls and I chosen to stay in our petty attitude of what he had not done to fulfill his parental duties and not traveled to be present with him, he would have died alone. Testimonial to the presence of our love and compassion, perhaps something had shifted for him. I like to think so! I do know for a fact that when an inner shift happens, an outer shift is soon to follow. The clichés for AIDS no longer held true for him: "Nobody cares," and "I am not good enough."

We flew half-way across the country on a moment's notice, thus, showing that we cared and that he was good enough. The circle was broken for him! We never regretted making that trip.

Honor Other People's Clichés—Don't Cross the Line

B ♫ Don't ever try to talk anyone out of their *fear-ful* beliefs/Clichés. One friend, because of one prior experience, created this cliché/belief for himself: "My car will break down when I go on a road trip." He no longer has the older car that was prone to break-downs, so it is logical to me that the fear would be gone—but in his mind it was still a very real fear. Even though he loved to travel, he seldom took a road trip and repeatedly took his car to the shop to check for problems.

Most people, because it is not their experience and subsequent fear, would say, "That's just silly, you shouldn't feel that way" or "just get over it that happened in the past." With my understanding of the Law of Attraction and the power of clichés, I would never try to talk anyone into taking action opposite of their fears, because I know the likelihood of their fear-based cliché manifesting. I usually make the comment, "If you have that concern then you should honor it." I knew that if I encouraged him to travel more, his fears could draw to him problems with his car. He will have to be the one to overcome his fear—this is another one of those personal "inside jobs!"

What Clichés Are We Teaching the Children?

L ♫ What clichés are we teaching the children, as a generation? Is it any wonder that we have whole generations that think alike? It is the job of each generation to filter out what doesn't work and be open to what does work.

Clichés That Just Pop-Up

Sometimes, things just pop right out of our mouths, without warning. More than once I have said in front of people, "I take that back," "I don't need to have an opinion about that," or "Let me rephrase that."

While working with clients, we always listened to their pop-up clichés. This gave us a clue as to what was happening in their lives and why. If they had an abusive father, this gave them the subconscious belief system that, "all men are abusive or cannot be trusted." This became their cliché, spoken or unspoken. Guess what type of men they drew into their lives? This made us ever more aware of our own clichés such as, "That blows my mind." The following story explains why!

Ponderism: *What if our Clichés came true—what then?*

This is a sad, but true story that gave me all the more reason to be aware of my thoughts. A friend of mine, who understood how clichés can help or hinder your life, kept me informed as this story unfolded. A friend of hers, who was a police officer that lectured in schools about being "Drug Free," is an excellent example of how a few habitual words can create devastation in our lives—*as a man thinks repeatedly so he becomes.*

Repeatedly, the officer talked to the children about being Drug Free. To get his point across, he would then point to the top of his head and the bottom of his chin, emphasizing "all that we are is between here and here." His intention was to help them use their minds to think and, thus, consciously choose not to use drugs. Unfortunately, his subconscious belief system took his cliché literally.

While handling his gun one day, it accidentally fired. According to the doctors, the bullet made the strangest movement they had ever seen. After entering the back of his head, the bullet changed directions—severing his spinal cord. Sadly, he was paralyzed from the neck down. He had become what he had often told the children—all that we are is between here and here.

The subconscious belief system is just that, "a system." As mentioned before, it does not rationalize what we tell it as right or wrong; its function is to carry out orders. Those orders are any repeated thought patterns, especially those with emotions.

Health Clichés

A lady came to me with stomach problems. The doctors could find nothing wrong with her. She was always upset about her life situations no matter how trivial—holding her captive in the "flight or fight" mode. She had spent a lot of money on remedies without finding a solution. After listening to her, I knew what the problem was; a cliché she repeated several times.

When talking about her life events she constantly said, "That makes me so sick." I advised her to stop saying the cliché, but each time she came back to see me, she continued to say it. For some people, their health issues are a way to get attention and, thus, feel loved. Because of this they, subconsciously, are not looking for a solution. I encouraged her to see someone else as I knew she was not ready to let go of her problem.

Here are some more health clichés. If you have leg problems: "I can't stand it." "I don't have a leg to stand on." "I can't stand up for myself." When someone says, "I have a pain in my neck," I usually ask, "Who do you know that is being a *pain in the neck?*" or "Are you being a *pain in the neck* to someone?" They have a surprised look on their face as they tell their story. I will not even think the thought "*you are a pain in the butt,*" because I don't want the consequences.

Here is an experience from one of our pre-published readers:

"I am enjoying your book very much! I want to share an experience I had that I know was a direct result of reading your book.

I work at the library and we were preparing to close for the day. We have a circulation staff worker who is very precise and a perfectionist, so it takes her much longer to complete her duties. Anyway, as I was leaving I expected her and the other two circulation people to leave with me as usual. She told me that they intended to stay 15 minutes after closing because it was too hectic to close and leave right away. I said okay and left.

On the way to my car I was thinking, "be allowing, be tolerant, law of allowing, law of tolerance—I can't believe this!" When I heard "I can't believe this," I immediately changed it to "I believe this!" It made me realize why I have had difficulty believing spiritual laws and concepts—my clichés.

So, thank you for writing this wonderful book! It truly is of service to truth seekers! Is the print copy available?"   L.M., Wailuku, Hawaii

Chapter 8

HOW TO HAVE THE PERFECT RELATIONSHIP

Karma at First Sight

L ♫ In his book, *Practicing the Power of Now,* Eckhart Tolle says that relationships have never had as much conflict or problems as they are having in these present times. He makes an interesting observation that makes one stop and think—*relationships were not designed to make us fulfilled or happy!* This certainly was in conflict with all the "live happily-ever-after" fairy tales that programmed our subconscious belief system (our B.S.). But Tolle states that problematic relationship can actually offer you spiritual growth if you can accept that this is its' true purpose.

When I read Tolle's books, and especially this concept, I thought, finally, someone had put into words what Brenda and I had been practicing for several years in relationships but were unable to explain it on paper—probably because we had not yet graduated from Relationships 101.

Of great interest to me, was the fact that Tolle outlines the basic principles that Spirit had taught us regarding relationships—we were *home schooled by the Holy Spirit* and, finally, did graduate from Relationships 101. This was all the validation I needed for Tolle's work. It confirmed that everyone has access to the same information from Spirit and can tune in to the same Source, just as we did.

Relieved, and in awe that Tolle was able to write this information with such clarity, I was prompted to hold book discussion classes based on his work, for a couple of years. I can certainly say, as it has been said, that the teacher learns the most.

From observing these classes, I began to realize how much people could benefit from our experiences. In this chapter, we offer some of our relationship stories as templates on how to use relationships for spiritual growth.

If you want to put your spiritual growth into warp speed, read this book in conjunction with Tolle's books, especially, *Practicing the Power of Now*, part two on "Relationship as Spiritual Practice." By combining Tolle's philosophy and our experiences, you will have the *how-to manual* on having the "perfect relationship."

Ponderism: *What purpose do relationships serve?*

The only guarantee that comes with a relationship is that you will have the opportunity for spiritual growth. Just where might we find that perfect relationship for growth? This is the easy part—simply look around and observe that *we are always in relationship with someone or something:* family, friends and foes, time, money, and even God. If you are still having problems finding the perfect one to start with, here's a hint, pick the problematic one.

Watch your consistent thoughts and feelings as they are the director of the quality of that relationship and how it manifests, outwardly, in your life. Keep in mind that our reality is shaped by our karmic-based subconscious belief system, explained in a previous chapter. Guess what? This is what we call *normal* life on a polarity-based planet. The good news is that our purpose for being here is to transcend this self-created karmic reality, both good and bad, and take the next evolutionary step—we're ready, how about you? Therefore, all relationships hold the potential for growth—why not put them to good use?

The beauty of using relationships for spiritual growth is that they ALWAYS bring a win-win situation for both parties, even if the other person never knew what hit them. I always give gratitude for each situation that Spirit inspired me to walk through, knowing that others were balancing a huge amount of their karmic debt, and benefiting from the interaction as much or more than I.

The last few years have produced some incredible tools to help bring understanding to many people about *what on earth is going on!* The documentary, *What the Bleep Do We Know?* and the movie and book, *The Secret*, teaches us how this karmic reality is created and gives many ways to change it, including a key factor—loving yourself.

A Course in Miracles (ACIM) views salvation (the healing of our karmic debt) and forgiveness as one and the same. *"God is Love"* and *"All the world of pain is not His Will."* Our part in this is to heal our mind—the mind that holds a false belief system that brings misery to the world.

"Salvation is my only function here...Salvation and forgiveness are the same. Then turn to Him Who shares your function here [problematic relationships], and let Him teach you that you need to learn to lay all fear aside, and know your Self as love which has no opposite in you." ACIM Lesson 99

Karmic Disclaimer

The experiences that we share in this chapter are our perceptions of what happened in our personal relationships. They were filtered through our own self-created karmic debt, for which our soul takes full responsibility to balance; the good, the bad, and the ugly. Should you choose to use this information to balance your karmic debt, we take no responsibility for the outcome—proceed at your own risk—your soul will love you for it!

Clearing the Relationship Fog

If you are looking for happiness or love and have been disappointed, then perhaps your relationships have been for spiritual growth. This might give a new understanding to those painful relationships and you may actually come to appreciate them, as we did. How many times has a seemingly bad experience turned out to be the best thing that could have happened to you?

As Brenda and I fine-tuned our skills in becoming detached observers—the Watchers of our life's situations—our relationship judgments began to shift because we had moved into understanding from our hearts' perspective. With this new agenda, the magnetic pull of the karmic fog from our relationships began to clear. With our focus shifting to observing our actions and reactions, we noticed the emotional pain of our usual pattern of "taking everything personally" began to diminish, and eventually, only the peace that comes with observation remained.

Unknowingly, most people have a self-serving, hidden agenda in their relationships—if I give you love you will give me something in return, i.e., acceptance, value, etc. This is what often passes for love. There can be no greater mistake than this, for the *true spirit of love is incapable of expecting or asking for anything.*

We have come to look at relationships as a mirror of life and use that reflection to tell us what we need most to learn or what we need to change within ourselves. Relationships then become a conscious barometer to show us where we are on our spiritual paths. This is a vital key to finding a more balanced relationship, where each partner supports the other in their spiritual growth regardless of the dynamics playing out in daily life. As a result, we take victimhood out of our relationship experiences and began to truly have what many coin as *the perfect relationship*—something that many are searching for.

Once we began consciously using our relationships for spiritual growth, we found ourselves trusting Spirit more and more. We trusted that we would never be given more challenges than we could handle—although at times we had our doubts. Accepting life's reflections as being our own creation was a big step. We were awakening from the *normal* karmic (natural evolution) life, ruled by our ego personality, to trusting our intuition—our True Nature (spiritual evolution.)

Who Do You Trust?

B ♫ The immature perceptions of my youth, my subconscious background music, thought that a woman's husband had all her answers. By pleasing him, she could *trust* that he would provide and take care of her, and as a result, naivety and chaos ruled. The Bible said that the husband was the head of the household, and my wedding vows were to *trust* and *obey.* I even questioned the goal of the male editors who put that one in the Bible, because Spirit was telling me something different.

This set a pattern of giving my power away in relationships and experiencing many hard lessons while playing the submissive role. The magnetic pull of this pattern of losing myself in a relationship was so strong that it always happened before I knew what hit me. It was years before I realized the Catch 22, waking up to the feeling that I had *sold my soul* for a temporary fix, and the resulting false sense of being loved, valued, and nurtured.

The desire to always please others filtered over into other relationships and carried the high price of losing my sense of self and thus my life purpose—

taking "me" out of my life. It wasn't until after my divorce, and the opportunity for another relationship, that I realized my *trust issues* had little to do with the other person. It wasn't as much about whether I could trust them as it was about trusting my own intuitive guidance.

The second time around, I knew for sure what I *didn't* want in a relationship, and I had learned to trust and love myself enough to say, "No" to anything even hinting at the dynamics of my prior relationship. The pain of the past had helped me to awaken and to become more of the observer of life, resulting in my ability to make better choices. My future would hold many tests to see if I had learned this lesson.

One test came with a short relationship just after my divorce. I felt the physical attraction—the magnetic pull—with this person, and, once again, I surrendered my power. The difference this time was that of my being more observant of the controlling relationship dynamics, while paying attention to my waking dreams. This time, I didn't fall asleep at the Karmic wheel. The *too accommodating disorder* (TAD) that can't say "no," was losing its grip on my life choices. Within a short time, I was getting intuitive messages that it was time to end this relationship.

The final message came one evening at his place when I had my head on his shoulder and, suddenly, the back of my pierced earring fell off. This was unusual (a waking dream alert) and I had the feeling that I should pay attention. I pondered the waking dream and its meaning—"back off" was the reply; something so simple, yet very difficult to do when you have the TAD disorder. This relationship was a TAD much because he was a TAD late, still living in the old dynamics of relationship patterns—attracting women who can't "say no." This woman was now awake and aware and aced the test!

Relationships: The Magic Mirror of Truth

"If you want to meet someone who can fix any situation you don't like, who can bring you happiness in spite of what other people say or believe, look in a mirror, then say this magic word: 'Hello'."

— Richard Bach, *Messiah's Handbook*

L ♫ Many people change partners, blaming their relationship problems on the other person. In changing partners, they think they will be free of the problem, only to find the new relationship has the same problematic theme as the old one.

You look in the mirror and your hair needs combing—you don't comb the mirror, you comb your hair. You automatically know where to go to make the changes. It works the same way in life, and then life becomes one big magic mirror on the wall. It then holds the image of everything you will ever want to know about yourself and, if used correctly, is a wonderful way to speed up your spiritual growth. *The Living Code* helps you decipher the messages in Life's Magic Mirror.

Mirror, mirror on the wall— it has the Truth, just make the CALL!

When viewing the mirror of life and gaining the information that it holds, you find yourself detaching from the dynamics of the relationship situation. You then become more interested in trying to figure out what life has presented in the mirror. You begin asking better questions, *"What can I learn from this situation and how can I perceive this differently?"*

When I read the Bible (KJV)verse, *"All things work together for the good of them that love God,"* I was given ample opportunities to practice it. My question became, *"Where's the good in this?"* My faith grew as the good was revealed and the reason for the chaos and apparent madness in my relationships. I learned to surrender what was revealed and allow whatever needed to happen—trusting that everything was working for my good. This awareness helped me step into compassion and true forgiveness.

"I am never upset for the reason I think." ACIM

This quote from *A Course In Miracles* (ACIM) workbook lesson, allows the reader to ponder the idea that those things in our life situations that upset us are often triggered by something from our past. We often view a present moment life event from the filters of our subconscious belief system which distorts Life's Magic Mirror.

Have you ever met someone that reminded you of a person from your past and you found yourself reacting to that person with the same respect or disrespect that you felt for the person from your past? *ACIM* workbook lesson six has the reader ponder this quote, "I am upset because I see something that is not there."

ACIM gives several mental exercises to repeat when you experience an upset in your life or when you have quiet time to ponder those people from the past that triggered a negative reaction in you. The Course says, *"The degree of the emotion you experience does not matter...even a slight twinge of annoyance is nothing but a veil drawn over intense fury."*

When remembering these people, the Course suggests repeating these words, *"I am not angry at _____ for the reason I think."* Or *"I am not afraid of _____ for the reason I think."*

"I am determined to see things differently." ACIM

The Course states, *"There are no small upsets. They are all equally disturbing to my peace of mind."* It is suggested that you search your mind to find whatever is distressing you. A most valuable and speedy tool to release this negative emotional pattern is the technique we have given in the following chapter called the "NOW Points." I have found this technique to be extremely helpful in bringing peace to a troubled mind. The powerful "NOW Points" technique is a great help to those studying the course in working with "forgiveness lessons," which is the overall goal of the Course.

The Course suggests that you search your mind for what upsets you. Then repeat one of the sentences below until you feel an attitude shift:

"I am determined to see_____[name of person] differently."

"I am determined to see_____[specify the situation] differently."

Handling Criticisms—Change Yourself to Change Your Relationship!

A good example of the Magic Mirror is observing when people become critical of you, perhaps for no logical reason. The mirror may be telling you that you are judging yourself or another. This is an important opportunity to take an honest look at yourself in order to make the necessary corrections and become aware of any self-criticism.

I use the Magic Mirror when my husband is critical of me. I do my best not to take it personally and begin observing my life—am I being critical of myself or am I criticizing others? Without fail, once I locate the true inner reason for his criticism and make the correction within myself, he stops the criticism without my having to say a word about it.

B ♫ I, too, had been learning from the Magic Mirror of life and knew that when I feel critical of my husband, to not say anything, because the issue wasn't about him. When I first recognized this pattern, I would stop and look within and asked how to see this differently. I realized that the core issue was about my own self-criticism and the need to forgive myself. I would then clear the energy of this emotional issue by using some of the techniques given in the following chapter. I always noticed that I stopped the criticism and, actually, would forget all about the issue. Even today, this always helps me to return to the "perfect relationship"—IT was all about me!

Ponderism: *Could this be the meaning behind the Bible verse that says, judge not lest you be judged?*

L ♫ In essence *it is all self-judgment!* The Law of Karma says that whatever you give or do to others returns to the sender. Furthermore, you can only judge in others what is in you; otherwise you will not even notice it. As the Bible (NIV) mentions, before you can make a righteous judgment, first make a correction within—"*...first take the plank out of your own eye, and then you will see clearly to remove the speck from your brother's eye.*" This is a good time to use the *Magic Mirror.*

If you will but listen when others talk and use the Magic Mirror concept, they will tell you a world of information about themselves, based on their opinions of others. A good example: A friend and I had read the same book and her comment was that she did not like the book because the author's ego was annoying to her. I said I did not get that impression at all and enjoyed the book. She had just told me about herself.

I usually don't pay any attention to this self-revealing information from my friends because it happens so often. The exception is when it sets off my internal alarm system. A business partner once told me that so-and-so was very cut-throat in business dealings with him. I logged this observation in my internal file on them, just as a precaution, and kept my eyes open.

Having this valuable tool can help you stay balanced and avoid negative situations and judgments, while using compassion and understanding toward other people's unconscious actions. Often, you can see it coming and choose not to participate in their unconscious conversation or situation. Today, we are experiencing *instant karma*, so we must be diligent in relationships that provide us with the opportunity to move quickly through our karmic debt, taking care to not create more karma. Instant karma means that the results of our thoughts, feelings and actions are coming back to us quicker.

Instant Thoughts Manifest Quickly

My husband, Tom, and I were sitting at a restaurant with some friends marveling at the low price of gas. It had reached an all time high, in many places, of $4-5 a gallon and was now, drastically, coming back down, just before the elections of 2008. We pondered the question: how long had it been since gas was as cheap as it is now—$1.46?

After we finished our lunch, my husband drove to work and I went to the store. He was following behind me, and at one point a pickup truck moved in between us. Tom called my cell phone to tell me that I would not believe what was on the bumper sticker of the truck between us: "Eight years ago when Bush was elected president gas was $1.46 a gallon."

Ponderism: *What if our conversation had been negative and had come back just as quickly? Do you suppose there are any "real" accidents or are they just time-released?*

B ♫ In the late 1970's, I was inwardly criticizing a friend's actions. Within one week, I noticed that I was doing the very deed I had criticized him for. This was a profound awakening moment for me, realizing that we can become what we judge—the beam was in my eye, not his and he was simply the reflective mirror for my awareness of my issue.

Dealing With Loneliness in Relationships

L ♫ Tom and I moved from the foot hills of Denver, Colorado, to Northern Arkansas, where I had been promised a job with a new project in the area. Upon arrival, we discovered that the project had been canceled. Due to the impoverished area, it was a couple of months before my husband found a job. The job was out of town, and he came home on the weekends.

Our close relationship made the separation very difficult, and living on ten acres in the middle of nowhere added to my growing loneliness. During the week, the only human contact for me was by phone—a cell phone was a luxury we could not afford.

My awareness of the loneliness was a new experience, having been raised with a twin. I observed that days would go by without hearing a human voice—a very odd experience. I now knew what isolation was and it certainly took a while to get used to.

Each time my husband left on Sunday afternoon, I felt the loneliness, depression, and helplessness of the situation. I knew the Magic Mirror was offering me a chance to work on loneliness and I needed to change my perception to get out of the pain. I started using some of the spiritual tools that we teach in our workshops—the "NOW Points," which are explained in the next chapter.

Brenda and her husband were coming for our birthday weekend in a few weeks. This was a perfect time to find out if I could balance the mental habit pattern of thinking I was lonely after everyone left.

Taking advantage of this opportunity, I began using the NOW Points every time I became aware of any thoughts and feelings of loneliness. While holding these acupressure points on my forehead, I began, in my mind, to play out the loneliness script, feeling as much of the heavy energy that I could feel around the situation. The second part of the balancing was to hold these points and imagine how it would feel not to be lonely when everyone left that Sunday afternoon—this was the difficult part.

As my birthday weekend approached, I knew this would be a barometer weekend for me. I would soon find out where I was on the emotional scale of loneliness. This was not a pass-or-fail test, but a marker on the scale telling me if there was more clearing to be done. A clue that this was already working came when my husband informed me that weekend, that his boss told him to keep one of the company's cell phones.

When the time of their departure came, I monitored my feelings as we said goodbye. I was elated! I felt absolutely no loneliness—not even a "ping!" This is confirmation that the tools worked and that I had just balanced a big chunk of emotional karmic pain from the past.

A Birthday Surprise—the Icing on the Cake!

After everyone left, a very peaceful state came over me—the loneliness feeling was gone! About dusk, I began to hear a dog barking just beyond the back yard by the pond. It sounded like a puppy barking. Someone must have dropped off an unwanted puppy, as was common in those Arkansas hills. I did not want the responsibility, at this time, of taking care of an animal and ignored the pitiful howling—hoping he would wander off.

It was almost dark, the barking had stopped for a little while, then I heard it again, but now it was at my back door. There was no getting around this one, so I turned on the light and saw this beautiful, healthy, eight-week-old, shepherd puppy going in circles, howling with fear. My heart melted and I knew I had to bring the shivering little puppy inside. He fell asleep on my lap and I called my husband with the news, not knowing what his reaction would be. I found it interesting that the only dog he would ever consider having was a shepherd, because they were so intelligent.

My initial resistance of having a dog continued until I realized that with having a puppy, the loneliness would be gone. I began to enjoy thoughts of training him like Lassie, from my favorite childhood TV show. I decided this was a birthday present from the Universe and a sign that I had healed my loneliness issues—I dared not send this present back.

I pondered—did the dog arrive because I had acknowledged and healed the "loneliness pattern?" Did this make room for a new (puppy) relationship to come into my life? It was a very interesting sequence of events as I pondered the impact of this situation. Would the dog have arrived if I had chosen to continue being lonely?

Six months later we moved to the town where my husband worked and had a fenced yard for the dog. When I healed my loneliness perception, my world shifted to accommodate it. I now had a town, my husband and a dog!

> *"The universe rearranges itself to accommodate*
> *your picture of reality."*   — *Anonymous*

Relationship Transitions; Unconscious to Conscious
—When Karma is King!

B ♫ In relationships, you will probably find yourself in trauma and drama of either playing the aggressor or the victim. Both of these roles are an indicator of unconscious relating. Both the movie and the book, *The Celestine Prophecy*, gave us valuable insights into the dynamics of the roles played out in unconscious relationships. These insights explained the primary roles in relationships—intimidator, interrogator, the aloof one, and the poor-me victim—and how to move past these dramas by asking your-self, "What can I appreciate about this person?"

I prayed for extra help in writing this part of "my story," reluctant to relive the journey of the unconscious karmic choices of my youth, a time when I was too emotionally sensitive and took everything too personally. I made choices then that are very foreign to who I am today. My former self was just a shadow of who I am today, and those experiences now seem like the fabric of a bizarre dream, still feeling very real but also fleeting. After my prayer, my intuition nudged me to open *A Course In Miracles* workbook; *"All things are lessons God would have me learn. I place the future in God's hands. The past is gone, the future is not yet. Now I am freed from both."*

Is Losing Oneself the Real Key to Finding One's True SELF?

B ♫ When I got married, the wedding vows reflected what the Bible and my upbringing had taught me—that the wife's job is to serve, trust, and obey, and all would be well. I believed that self-sacrifice was the key to feeling loved and having a sense of value and purpose. As mentioned earlier, my husband's desires and goals always superseded my own because, after all, he would always have my best interest at heart—or so my naïve unconscious self thought. Ultimately, I learned that living in the unconscious web of another's dreams and goals wasn't the key to happiness, for either of us. Having no personal boundaries, I often felt confused, alone, and afraid.

The *Celestine Prophecy* helped me to understand our roles; he was the intimidator and interrogator, and I played the poor-me victim role, which was a mirror-image of my relationship with my mother. This often left me feeling trapped, small, and inadequate.

As mentioned previously, we were not raised with affection or praise lest we become vain and, thus, sinners. By puberty I was so in need of affection that I latched onto one of the two boys available at the small country church, (We were only allowed to date boys of our faith.) and was grateful that he was even interested. I realized that if I looked sexy I would get his attention, and this gave me a sense of value that I had never felt before; the "sex kitten" years began. After a very rocky courtship, I married right out of high school and moved to another state.

Within the first hour of saying, "I do," I saw a side of my new husband that I didn't know existed; karmic unconscious love is truly blind. Something didn't please him and to my shock and dismay, he threw a temper tantrum with a stream of profanity I had never heard him utter before.

I will never forget the sinking feeling in the pit of my stomach, a feeling that I had just made a huge mistake. I felt trapped, because our mother often said, "You make your bed, you have to lie in it," and my commitment to marriage was also heavy on my mind…"trust and obey." Had I just "jumped out of the frying pan into the fire?" It would be many years before I realized this was actually the cleansing fire of Spirit that would eventually lead the way to my salvation—freedom and the kingdom within.

In the first six months of married life, I had several "wake-up calls." One was that he told me that his wedding ring gave him a rash and he decided to stop wearing it. Today, this waking-dream would have told me volumes about the road ahead.

Wife Swapping—Was This the Solution to My Problem?

He decided that I had a real problem when it came to sexual desire, which I did, and he thought he knew how to fix my problem. I was naive enough to think he was right—*Men Are from Mars and Women Are from Venus* by John Gray, had not been written yet. Coming from a home that never addressed sex and having the impression that the body was "dirty," it was a really difficult topic for me to discuss.

Even though I tried to look sexy and did the "blonde thing" (the Marilyn Monroe look), it wasn't about sexual feelings for me, it was about receiving attention and feeling valued. He decided, and convinced me, that the solution to solve my sexual problem was to have sex with other men—what did I know?

In the 1970's, when the faddish concept of wife-swapping came around, this seemed the next natural step to "fix" my problem. He failed to understand that most women take intimacy very personally, and a couple of times I fell in love with the other person. This, too, was very hard to deal with because, inside, a battle raged, while outside I had to play the part of a "happily married" woman who was now truly "sexually evolved." Any attempt to discuss my unhappiness with my husband only started another control drama, to which I always gave in, because I still felt responsible for his happiness.

Little did I understand at the time that I was learning valuable lessons in humility, tolerance, compassion, and unconditional love that would eventually set both of us free. He played his part perfectly in my Divine Plan—to help me awaken from my hypnotic slumber, and for that I shall be eternally grateful. He helped me define the *perfect relationship*—we don't know what we want until we have lived what we *don't* want.

It Is All About Me!

For years I pondered a deeper meaning to my relationship challenges. In the 1980's, the understanding came in a vivid past-life dream. The dream explained that I had been my husband's controlling mother and had the same sexual addictive habits he showed today. It explained why I often felt more like his mother than his wife and that I was reaping what I had unconsciously sown in another lifetime. The karmic wheel had to be balanced. These very humbling insights moved me into more compassion and forgiveness; it wasn't about him, *it was all about me!* I now understand why I stayed in the marriage, why I played the victim role, and forgiving myself and him was the key to my freedom. This relationship created the resistance I needed to wake up!

Where's the Girl I Married?

After twenty-plus years of marriage, my waking-dreams were telling me that my departure was close at hand. I knew I had done my homework when my husband asked, "Where's the girl I married?" Of course he was referring to the one that felt responsible for his happiness, sacrificed her needs over his, and felt more like a "mother" than a wife. I simply replied, "She grew [woke] up." My "too accommodating disorder" (TAD) was beginning to heal.

The Final Battle With Jealousy—the Mile High City

L ♫   I pondered what a relationship would be like if the pattern of jealousy was not a part of my life experiences. I became a *hound of heaven* to set myself free of this painful issue.

Several months later, through synchronistic events, I found myself on the way to Denver on a Friday the 13th (a lucky day for me) in the late summer of 1999. I was now in a new relationship that felt different from all the others. I did not feel the strong sexual magnetic pull toward this person, as in past relationships. I took this as a good sign—strong sexual magnetism smacks of a karmic lesson—which is great for spiritual growth if you can stay conscious through it. I was getting a little weary by now and was hoping that this person would play the final part in my ongoing jealousy conspiracy—would this be the one to set me free?

Over the years, using clearing techniques to balance the emotional energy as they surfaced, has helped me, in many situations, to be more objective. This allowed me to keep the emotions of jealousy at bay and remain silent when a jealousy moment arose. I learned to hold my peace, and then in a private place (sometimes even a public bathroom) I would balance the emotional energy that had come up.

Just like clockwork, another opportunity would be just around the corner—I shed many tears while peeling off the layers of this pattern. On several occasions I was not sure who was winning; it depended on how much my mind wanted to chew on the situation.

Since I had learned to keep silent about the jealousy issues, this new relationship had more harmony in it than I had ever known. Balancing the negative karmic energy daily (renewing the mind daily, as the Bible calls it) kept it from building up and creating a "mountain out of a molehill."

The final battle came Thanksgiving Day when my partner's ex-wife was invited to the family Thanksgiving Dinner. I pondered if this would truly be a day of Thanksgiving—what did Spirit have in store for me?

This was the first time I had met his ex-wife. She seemed very pleasant and non-threatening. As I listened to my partner and her engrossed in conversation for what seemed like hours, I began to observe the emotions of jealousy arising.

As if there were two of me in the same body, this energy (or entity) came at me with a vengeance, literally trying to consume me. I watched as the negative feelings became stronger and stronger. Thank God I had learned to hold my peace, because the observer in me realized that my partner had not given me any reason to be jealous, but my mind or this "spirit of jealousy" wanted to convince me otherwise. I felt the energy so intensely at one time that the room seemed darker and farther away, and I felt faint. I could have left the room but did not feel inclined to do so; actually, I was almost glued to the floor as if possessed.

I exhausted every tool I knew, trying to end the barrage of energy that was besieging me. Finally, I settled on visualizing the White/Christ Light at my feet coming up slowly through my body and back down. I stayed focused on running this energy while my emotional body was going ballistic, as if possessed by a foreign entity. In almost a decade of doing energy balancing, I had never encountered anything like this before. This spirit of jealously had met its match—my Taurus bullheadedness was going to stick with it until the end. I knew I must be getting close to ending this jealousy wrestling match for it to come on this strong.

The True Battle of Armageddon

I have come to the conclusion that the so-called Battle of Armageddon is really an inner battle, such as the one I experienced, and deals with the two forces the Bible calls the carnal mind/ego (outer) and the spiritual mind (inner) seeking balance on a polarity-based planet—it's all about living a balanced life.

As a child, I had an active imagination about how hell would feel—because of this experience I finally realized that I did not have to die to go to hell. I knew, firsthand, what hell felt like as this battle constantly raged within my mind. For seven days I could not get my mind to stop going over and over this "Thanksgiving Day" event, even to the point of not being able to sleep because of it…*my mind had a mind of its own.*

Because of the intensity, I knew this was the final hour of the battle and my Taurus hooves dug in for the final pull with the inner knowing that Spirit would give me the strength to win if I did not give up. As a last resort, I began repeating different power-charged words—this was not even something I would normally do, so it had to be inner-directed. Somebody was hearing my calls for help.

On the last day of the seven-day barrage of inner chatter, I climbed the walking path in the foot hills of Denver just above where we lived. I reached a rock I liked to sit on that had a wonderful view of Denver. I began allowing charged words to come to me and would repeat them with great emotional fortitude when, suddenly, a great calm came over me and I let out a sigh of great relief. Finally, the battle was over—victory was mine! I felt exhausted. I felt an unusual shift in my energy field, as if a weight lifted off my shoulders—could it possibly be that the spirit of jealousy had indeed possessed me and was now gone?

The next several months were interesting and brought many changes. I began observing, with awe, situations that normally would have stimulated a jealous reaction in me, but the feelings were just not there. Instead, a freedom and peace of mind I had never felt before had taken their place.

Even now, Brenda and I do not tell people about our wonderful supportive relationships with our husbands/partners—they simply would not believe it. My pondering question of what a relationship without jealousy would be like has been answered. It has been worth the inner struggle to gain freedom from those emotional bars that held me prisoner for so many years, and perhaps many lifetimes.

Anyone reading this book will probably not have to go through the intensity that I did. I feel that many of our stories have a double purpose: for our spiritual growth and for sharing them in this book. I know that when each person does their best to balance a karmic debt, involving such issues as jealousy, they not only help themselves, but this makes it easier for the next person—as Jesus said, *"As I am lifted up, so are you."* It's like blazing a trail so others can follow—not you, personally, but the trail.

Exercise for a conscious relationship: If my husband says something or does something that upsets me, I don't say anything to him until I have balanced the emotional energy within myself. Then if I feel it necessary, I share it with my husband. By that time, I am in a non-emotional place I can easily talk about it without being upset. This is such a freeing experience and usually brings us closer together.

When my husband gets upset, I do my best to stay present, not getting emotional about what he is saying. In this way, I am not adding any negative energy to his and creating a monster that we will have to deal with later. I have found this to be a very effective way to work through issues quickly.

Karma at First Sight
—We Have the Good, the Bad, and Then It All Gets ugly!

*"When life is 'falling apart' things could actually be falling together...
maybe for the first time."* — Neale Donald Walsch

A common experience in many new relationships is the karmic magnetism of *love-at-first-sight* or *head-over-heels-in-love* experiences. People
want "fireworks," and/or "bells and whistles," but after the fireworks are gone
it can become a love/hate relationship. What we think is love-at-first-sight
could be the magnetic pull of our karmic debt. Some who are able to work
through this debt together find a more compatible relationship, while others
go their separate ways.

Magnetic Attraction—When the Honeymoon is Over!

L ♫ When I divorced the second time, I was much more aware of the
compulsive magnetic behavior that happens when one is single again. This
behavior will express in various ways, such as losing weight when one could
never do it while married, dressing more attractively, going to the gym, etc.
Without knowing it, these are all symptoms of frantically searching for another
partner. Having experienced this myself, I know it is as if something is lacking
until I find the right person to make me feel complete.

What is actually happening is a *magnetic dance*. You feel "less than"
and go in search of the feeling of wholeness. The partner you choose fits the
magnetic frequency with which you are in sync—you like their vibes. For a
while, you are excited and feel the wholeness you are looking for, depending
on how long the "honeymoon" lasts. Many women feel they just have to have
a man in their lives, and vice versa. In actuality, energetically they feel less
than—incomplete—without the energy of a partner. The intensity of this will
vary among different people.

When you partner with another person this magnetic dance shifts your
energy. Like the north and south poles of the magnet coming together, you
have a feeling of wholeness and are no longer looking for another magnetic
match. The true test comes after the "honeymoon" is over and you settle into
who you each were before the relationship started. This is the time you will

know if your magnetic attraction is still a match or if you are in a karmic dance of opposites.

I had my first experience with karmic magnetism when I was dating in high school. Often, on Sunday night after church, a bunch of us kids would pile into a car and go cruising. I sat by one of the boys that happened to be a couple of years younger than me. As we rode in the car, he put his arm around my shoulder. This was the first time I literally felt magnetic attraction—as if we were opposite sides of a magnet coming together. I spent the rest of the evening fighting off this extremely strong energy-urge to put my head on his shoulder. I had never felt anything like this before, but in spite of the magnetic pull, I knew this was not the relationship for me.

B ♫ Thank God our life lessons were different. By sharing each of our experiences we had a 360-degree view of relationships, and that by learning from each other's experiences we reduced our own karmic debt.

Boundary Issues and Blondie Issues

Ponderism: *Are boundary issues in relationships what keeps us bound?*

B ♫ My primary issue in relationships was that of not having boundaries; I couldn't say "no." This "dis-ease to please" carried over into all other areas of my life. I shied away from confrontations because I had no voice when it came to standing up for myself. Yet, as with everything, there is always a positive side to view and my "aim to please" did benefit me in becoming an exceptional employee, which resulted in good promotions.

In my mid-twenties I began to read self-help books, which at that time there weren't very many. As the years went by, I began the long journey in learning to love and appreciate myself. After my divorce and the move back to Missouri, I began to dress differently; the sex-kitten aspect of my need for men's approval to feel value was diminishing. I no longer wanted to be the object of the male "lust looks," or to play the part of the "dumb (naïve) blonde."

My final encore came one day when, once again, I decided to wear one of my shorter skirts. After work, I ran an errand at a local store where I had an experience that is still crystal clear in my mind. I vividly remember looking down the aisle to the other end of the store where a man in a white shirt stood staring at me. I suddenly felt a blast of uncomfortable energy coming my way. Interestingly, this energy used to make me feel good about myself because I felt acknowledged, and now—for the first time ever—I felt repulsed! This was my first awareness of an actual physical sensation in feeling the energy dynamics of this dense, lower-vibration energy—lust looks. Blehhh!!

Was I now magnetically repelling the "neediness" energy that, before, had held me bound in its karmic magnetic pull? This was a force to be reckoned with, and one to which I couldn't say "no." Did my learning to love/appreciate myself create an invisible shield in the form of new boundaries—was the "dumb blonde disorder" taking its next evolutionary step?

As I came to view all of my life experiences as "lessons God would have me learn," I came to appreciate and look at what I learned from my "blonde experiences." I knew that I had just worked or drudged through what felt like lifetimes in this karmic pattern—I learned to focus on and be grateful for my spiritual lessons in humility, tolerance, and compassion for myself and others.

This experience even prompted me to eventually change my platinum blonde hair color, returning it to my "natural state"—the blonde awakened. My motto had always been, "the smart blonde just plays dumb." Was it time to *stop playing small*? For me, changing my hair color, symbolized getting back to my true nature—the next time I go blonde it will be different—*conscious blonding.*

Conscious Relating

When we respond to our evolutionary plan in life, we stop following our old choices—we feel whole within ourselves.

Today, Linda and I are grateful that both of us, and our husbands, consciously worked to balance enough of our karmic debt that we all have a more harmonious partnership. Our "later in life" marriages don't carry the magnetic karmic pull. Through other relationships we all learned to define what we did and didn't want in a relationship, and then the Universe brought to each of us someone that carried our new definition—the new vibes.

By allowing prior relationships to be our teachers and leave behind resentment and judgment, we were each free to choose again. We now have a deeper loving relationship than any of us have experienced before —we and our partners are free to be our true selves.

Ponderism: *Why and how do we leave the "perfect relationship?" Can we really leave a relationship in a spiritual way without creating more karma?*

L ♫ When your partner no longer "pushes your buttons" you are free to leave the relationship if you choose. Otherwise, you will attract another karmic, magnetic relationship mirroring the one you just left. The illusion in relationships is that you think a new person will be different but, unless you have changed yourself from the inside out, your relationship won't change either. Many people learn this the hard way through many relationships— don't judge yourself for having several relationships; they all serve a spiritual purpose. When you heal from the inside out, you are balancing the karmic scale. This eliminates the proverbial question, *"Why do I keep attracting the same personality types in my relationships?"*

As our frequencies shift through our self-healing/forgiveness, we may find people coming and going in our lives. If they are no longer needed to reflect anything back to us, they may move out of our lives. I found this to be true when I realized I had stopped reacting to my preacher husband's temper tantrums, even though I had no clue as to what would set them off.

Out of self-preservation and total frustration, one day I found myself going into a surrendered state of extreme peace. From then on I went into that state of peace each time his anger flared. My state of peace just provoked more anger from him. Within two months he was gone. The karmic magnetic circuit was broken.

Brenda also dealt with the temper tantrums of her first husband. As she acknowledged her own inner anger and healed from within, she also became non-reactive to his control dramas. Growing up, we were not allowed to express our feelings or opinions. Unknowingly, we held them inside, especially those of anger and frustration. In relationships we found it difficult to express our true feelings, not knowing when it would meet with disapproval and set off another tantrum.

Brenda Leaves the *Perfect Relationship*

B ♫ After I had been married for fifteen years, I decided that it was time to leave. I knew that even though it would be tight, I could finally support myself financially. For the first time, I felt empowered in our relationship and expressed my unhappiness to my husband. To my surprise his heart was open, because I think he knew I meant it. He promised to change and told me a sad childhood story that explained his anger, which had been out of control for the last fifteen years. As I pondered his promises, I also became aware that I was still attracted to men with similar personalities and would, most likely, end up in a similar situation if I left him—my karmic (forgiveness) lessons weren't over. I decided to stay and try one more time, and it was different for a while.

After twenty-six years, the karmic scales were balanced and it was now time to leave the "perfect relationship." I had learned to love both of us unconditionally, and to appreciate him for being a master teacher for my spiritual growth—my spiritual awakening. I related my "conscious exit" story in chapter five, explaining that I knew six months beforehand that I would be leaving and how my every step was directed by the Holy Spirit's guiding hand. I had a subtle knowing that for both of us to grow spiritually, I needed to leave, and that to stay would be *spiritual death*—so staying was no longer an option as it had once been.

Miraculously, I was able to keep my focus on the goal, which kept me out of fear and doubt. By staying in the present moment—staying conscious—I could easily hear the calm, still voice within, and this was a vital key to helping me stay out of doubt and fear. Every day I asked, "What do I need to do today, regarding my exit?" Without fail, the answer came. I simply had to follow Spirit's lead.

Because I took that leap of faith, I saw miracles happen and, today, I look back and ponder—who was that masked woman? I went to the top of the mountain and saw the varmint—the varmint was me—it was all about *me* after all!

Linda left her second husband a few months after I came to live with her. Not until we were writing this chapter did we realize we both left our marriages for the same reason. Each of us had received inner guidance that for everyone to continue growing spiritually, we needed to leave—to stay would be "spiritual suicide."

My Husband's Experience with His Spiritual Growth

L ♫ I was fascinated when my husband, Tom, told me that through the years, before we met, he also learned to look at everyone around him as an aspect of himself—although he didn't call it the Magic Mirror.

Recently, he shared a story about a former boss that reminded him of his father, who is now deceased. They even had the same hair color and mannerisms. When my husband was around him, he noticed that his boss often brought up the same uncomfortable feelings he had felt with his dad. One day the feeling was very intense, but Tom was able to stay in the Watcher mode and work at balancing his emotions as they came up, trying to stay at peace. What was interesting to him was how the situation resolved itself, once he made peace within.

So, *a partner for spiritual growth does not always have to be the person that originally pushed your buttons*. In this case, it was interesting that it was someone who reminded him of his father, although his boss was much younger. My husband was pleased that he could balance the karmic scale with his father, even though his father was not present. He no longer has this person for a boss—an indicator to him that something has shifted within himself.

Finally, the Conscious Relating!

We have both come to the following conclusions. The only bad relationship is one where you chose not to grow spiritually. In our case, we out-grew several relationships as the other person opted to stay where they were. We are now in relationships where our partners are growing with us. Our direction in life is Spiritual growth; no more no less!

The Morning After

We worked on this chapter mostly during a period referred to, in Astrology, as Mercury Retrograde, and wanted to have it finished during this three-week time-frame since it was a good time for editing; reviewing the past. On the last day of Mercury doing its backward journey in the Zodiac, which can create miscommunication, electronic problems, and delays, we still had to finish the end of this chapter, and Brenda had to rewrite her last story. Our experiences on that day reflected typical Mercury Retrograde energies and demonstrated the powerful bond between twins.

B ♫ As we were completing this chapter, unknown to the other, we each had significant dreams that would guide the way to completing what seemed like our most important part yet. I could feel myself procrastinating in getting my part done, which is a familiar signal that always tells me something significant is trying to release. At one point, I felt guilty that my schedule had permitted me to contribute only my personal stories to this chapter.

After we shared our dreams, my guilt left as I realized why Linda had to write the opening, because I was to finish it. My dreams indicated that I was doing the inner work of transmuting heavy energies—almost from the beginning of our writing this chapter. I noticed that I often had to stop and do an emotional clearing while writing.

Thank God for a Spirit-led sister who inwardly held my emotional stress-release points during our editing process, which brought me back into balance. Not until the experience of the following dreams and my discussing them with Linda did I realize how significant this chapter was for me.

The next morning, after Mercury Retrograde ended, I was wide awake at 4:00 a.m. and, amazingly, I felt great and full of energy. I got up, grateful for the extra time to meditate and write down the dreams that felt significant. In pondering their meaning, I realized they had to do with my section of this chapter. After my meditation, I started receiving a key point that wasn't apparent the day before.

Miraculously, this part of the book that felt like a struggle the day before, now flowed with ease and grace—the sign I look for in spiritual writing. This lightness carried an inner vitality and a sense of well-being that stayed with me most of the day.

This particular morning I was excited to share these dreams and insights with Linda, and I knew she would enjoy Spirit's humor. She hadn't Skyped me for our usual 7:00 a.m. appointment, so I knew we had a miscommunication. I hoped that she was sleeping in and enjoying the morning off. I was grateful because this had given me the perfect amount of time to finish my section.

Brenda's Dream the Morning After

The dream started in a room with a man and a woman who had just completed grueling work on a movie set. The man had a little recuperation time, but the woman was completely exhausted. None of us fully realized how much energy it would take for them to finish their parts in this movie, especially the woman. I felt a complete new respect for all actors in general.

I knew as I was writing down this dream that the movie was my "life movie—my story" being played out, and both the man and the woman represented unfamiliar aspects of myself. This told me that I had just completed something important, which had obviously taken a lot more energy than I realized. Not until sharing it with Linda did all the pieces fall together. I began grasping that it had to do with the heavy emotions that she helped me clear the day before, while finishing my part of this chapter. Now I knew why I felt freer and lighter this morning.

The dream immediately following that one, found me preparing to enter the back seat of a beautiful, expensive sedan. The car door required a key for entry and an unfamiliar woman appeared with a key. Upon opening the door, she gave me an affectionate kiss that didn't seem out of place. My attention was then drawn to a place behind her where people were gathering, seemingly waiting for us. End of dream.

I knew this dream represented my physical vehicle and was pointing out my renewed sense of well-being. The woman with the key was a new aspect of myself that held the key to open new doors for me. The emotional release that Linda helped me with the day before was "key" to my union (the kiss) and, thus, an emotional healing. Linda suggested that the people waiting behind the woman were all the people who would be helped by this story. Our final edit brought further insights about the kiss and the people waiting.

Linda's Dream the Morning After

L ♫ I slept in until 6:00 a.m. and awoke after a haunting dream. I was grateful for the time this morning to meditate and process this dream, since Brenda and I would not be getting together—so I thought. I went to bed thinking how wonderful it was to be finished with my part of this chapter since I knew our pattern and it was working well for us; it was Brenda's job to finish this chapter.

My Dream: I was with a group of people helping to prepare for a wedding. I kept putting the ceremony off because of one more thing I thought needed to be done. Anxiously, I realized how late it was; almost midnight. We were at the eleventh hour, you might say, and no ceremony—in my mind this was not good. The next morning, I gathered everyone together and said, "Let's get this show on the road"—everyone laughed. I felt a little guilty, thinking that the night before should have been the honeymoon night. End of dream.

I knew this dream was important to finishing this chapter during Mercury Retrograde, and it left me with an anxious feeling that we had not finished our jobs on time. Little did I know the ceremony could not be completed until I joined—in union—with Brenda, and we put together the pieces of what just happened as related next.

When the phone rang about 7:30 that morning, I knew I was in trouble. Brenda humorously said, "Where are you? I have been writing since five a.m."

As we excitedly began to share our dreams, the relevance of the synchronicity of our miscommunication about our meeting and the dreams began to make more sense—ALL was in perfect timing—Divine Order.

We felt that Linda's procrastination in her dream was probably due to taking the time, periodically, to help Brenda clear her emotional issues relating to this chapter, which was holding things up. Linda's anxious feelings in her dream reflected her desire to finish this chapter during Mercury Retrograde.

In Linda's dream the union, or ceremony, finally did take place and she was actually dreaming it while Brenda was awake and writing her part at 5:00 a.m. Could it have been that the kiss, or union, in Brenda's dream represented the ending to Linda's ceremony, the luxury sedan was the wedding car, and the people behind the woman in Brenda's dream were the wedding guests in Linda's dream, watching the ceremony at the car?

B ♫ Not until talking with Linda did I fully realize the magnitude of how emotionally healing writing my part of this chapter had been. As I looked back over my dream journal, I realized that, at the beginning of Mercury Retrograde, I also had begun a new clearing mediation exercise—Healing from the Heart. The content of my dreams, at the beginning and the ending of the three-week period, told me the significance of the clearing exercises and our work together.

With that said, I literally stood up and "danced a jig." Linda could hear me through her computer speakers, tap dancing on my desk mat with shouts of joy—my non-traditional salvation was at hand! The inner child was back and ready to go!

Chapter 9

PUTTING YOUR SPIRITUAL HOUSE IN ORDER

Clearing the Karmic Clutter

"The goal of the curriculum, regardless of the teacher you choose, is 'know thyself'. There is nothing else to seek."   — *A Course In Miracles*

"Do not count on anything except what is within you."
— Buddha

In this chapter we share some very effective exercises that have helped us; "deal with it"—life's challenges. These exercises are helpful in clearing the clutter that resides hidden in the subconscious mind. Once you understand the information in this book, then you will realize that you are the only one responsible for getting your house in order—*know thyself*.

"When you know who you are, then, you know who you are not."

L ♫ According to quantum physics, we have infinite possibilities to choose from at each crossroad moment in life's journey. Once we begin to make conscious (better) choices, our lessons will have greater purpose because we are willing to take responsibility for any and all results. I now believe there are no wrong choices. I have truly experienced the reality that all things work together for the good of those who love God—sometimes there is a time delay before we see the good—but it is there!

We have used the word *house* in the chapter title as a metaphor regarding our state of consciousness, and the many levels of awareness that goes with it. It has been Humanity's evolutionary path to focus its consciousness on the outer life—our DO-ing. We are in the midst of an evolutionary shift—it is NOW time to focus on our inner life—our BE-ing. We have been told for two-thousand years to seek the inner kingdom—the Kingdom of Heaven. Simply put, we are to shift our awareness (focus) from where we are now to a new state of consciousness, by renewing the mind daily.

Anything that does not vibrate in harmony with this new awareness cannot survive the coming accelerated shift in consciousness and must be left behind. This includes the garbage (dysfunctional thoughts) held in our subconscious mind, from all prior programming—karmic clutter. We can either clean the clutter of this karmic debt or it will be cleaned for us. Personally, I would rather do it myself than have the "cosmic two-by-four" wake-up call that many are experiencing today.

The book, *The Celestine Prophecy* by James Redfield and more graphically, the movie, gives an excellent overview of this new state of consciousness we are seeking. The main character, John, had no clue as to what he was seeking, which is typical of Humanity today. As you will see, it was his/our destiny to find the answers—driven by an inner impulse that is unquenchable. Toward the end of the story, the character, Will, helps others move into this new state of awareness by shifting their thoughts, and they realized that by stepping out of their fears, *nothing could harm them unless they allowed it.*

In Redfield's work, you will learn more about the sign posts—the inner guidance given along the invisible HIGHER-way to a new spiritual home (a new state of consciousness). His information on following your intuition greatly complements our chapter on dreams and waking-dreams.

Another helpful book in understanding how our childhood program-ming, our subconscious belief system, controls our lives is, *The Biology of Belief* by Dr. Bruce H. Lipton, a renowned cell biologist. Lipton has done an amazing job of connecting science and spirituality. He learned through a muscle testing experience with a chiropractor that the subconscious belief system is in control. Muscle testing is something that we have taught for years as a valuable tool to identify our negative subconscious beliefs.

Lipton further explains that when we are not totally focused in the present moment, the subconscious mind is managing our affairs the way it was programmed. This explains why all our efforts with positive affirmations may not seem to work. Even though we are affirming something positive, there may be an unconscious old program still running, that is in control. This truly explains that we all live by the Grace of God.

Lipton also explains that it is almost futile to use willpower to try to overcome this programming. We agree and have had great success personally with reprogramming our subconscious beliefs by utilizing the exercises mentioned in this chapter and taught in our workshops.

Do We Really Want to Take on the Job of Cleaning Other People's Houses?

Ponderism: *Can we really know what is best for another? Do we think we can clean their house without getting some of their dirt/karma on us?*

"You do not know what others really need. The trials they face belong to the path that is theirs to tread. Therefore avoid lamenting their problems... The best help you can give your fellow man is to seek inner strength within yourself. Go your own way in faith and prayer. These are the keys for recognizing the direction to take...You will see the awakening, the approach of a new life beyond the chaos."
— Trigueirinho

We all want to help others, especially our loved ones. It is easy to stand on the sidelines and yell directions: you should do this and your life will be great! I have learned to ponder my motives before giving aid of any kind; am I giving aid based on their actual needs or what I, emotionally, think is best for them?

My experience has been that I usually come to regret an action based on an emotional decision. If time permits, I wait for an inner impulse—those reoccurring nudges. If no inner direction comes, I do the best I can and, if at all possible, I do nothing and wait—sometimes no action is the best action. Many times the situation resolves itself, if I stay out of the way.

I have come to a greater understanding of what the Master Jesus meant by *the poor you have with you always*. I now know that unless we can help someone change their subconscious negative programming, they will never have enough and we can never give them enough money, time, love, or anything else. If they have a built-in self-saboteur (the subconscious B.S.) living within themselves, then it will override all of our best intentions. The "Now Points" given in this chapter will help clear some of that clutter as it arises.

This doesn't mean you can't do *something*, but you must realize that the *something* might involve *allowing* them their experience—this is the greatest form of love that you can give them. You love them enough to allow them to experience what they need for spiritual growth. This is not an easy path to follow but it is the quickest for all concerned, especially for parents, unless it involves the child's safety—conscious parenting *(The Biology of Belief)*. If you can do this, you will feel spiritually empowered and spiritually humbled at the same time—what a dichotomy!

As I worked with this concept in my life, this realization finally came. The angel/spiritual guide of the person I am trying to help is in control and knows what is needed more than I do. I just needed to learn to trust. Who am I to question the path their angels have laid for them—who do you think knows best for them, you or God? Often the best action is surrendering to *what is*, and this can open the door for miracles to happen. A very good self-help book on this is, *Loving What Is* by Byron Katie.

For a long time I stopped praying for people until I could understand how to pray correctly. If you want to say a prayer for someone else it is okay to ask for what you want, but then surrender your desire for them by saying something like, "Not my will be done but Yours." Go into acceptance of what is, knowing that all is in Divine Order just the way it is.

Pondering is another form of prayer and is an excellent way to bring Higher Truth into our lives. How open we are to receiving new information will determine the depth of the Truth we receive.

If you really want to be of service to others, the best place to begin is to put your own spiritual house in order—*work out your own salvation by getting to "know thyself."*

"It is not necessary to worry about how to pray. What is important is to open ourselves to our Inner Being with our attention and our sincerity... Prayer is to love the Inner Being and to seek it constantly...The key to true prayer is to seek ones Inner Being in the truest, most complete and natural way."
— Trigueirinho

Putting Your Spiritual House in Order

Ponderism: *Is getting to know who you are a part of getting your house in order?*

B ♫ Since this is truly an inside job, no one can clear your clutter for you any more than they can digest your food. Others can help you, but only when you are committed too.

As I look back over my spiritual journey, I can see the "sign posts" along the way. The visions in my twenties telling me to love God with all my heart, love my neighbor as myself, and to seek first the kingdom of God, are lifelong Ponderisms, and were vital keys to putting my spiritual house in order.

Then, the surreal dream telling me there was more truth than what was in my Bible prompted the necessary questions for me to ask, allowing me to get out of the "box" of my past religious teachings. These teachings of my youth weren't working for me as they had for my family. *I was living in their spiritual house, not mine.*

L ♫ We are in wonderful times because of the many opportunities that soul brings our way to clear the clutter from our house/mind. We do not have to go looking for problems to solve; all that we will ever need for this house cleaning is what is in our life at this very moment—and for most of us, that is plenty to keep us busy. If you pursue this path, then you won't have much time to clean another's house.

The following techniques come from our years of experience with personal clients, family, friends, and workshops.

The Spiritual Technology to Stay in Balance
—When You are Knee-Deep in Clutter!

L ♫ Unresolved stress is the underlying cause of many physical, emotional, and mental health issues as, *The Biology of Belief*, has scientifically proven. Lipton clearly explains how stress "severely compromises your vitality."

Emotional Stress Technique

In the 1990's, I became a workshop instructor for an alternative health care modality called, *Touch for Health Kinesiology.* It introduced me to the following emotional stress release technique that I call the *NOW Points Technique.* I have found it to be one of the most valuable tools I have taught and experienced personally to help myself and others release emotional stress; it works great every time.

This acupressure technique is very easy to learn and to teach to others. It works especially well with children. Every child should be taught how to use the NOW Points to release any emotionally upsetting event, especially one that has just happened. Mothers tend to do this naturally when a child is sick, as she lovingly strokes the child's forehead. These acupressure points are connected to the stomach energy flow/meridian and, thus, relaxes and calms the child.

The NOW Points help release the negative energy stored in the body, caused by our emotional response to challenging situations. As we mentioned before, on a subconscious level trauma is still circulating and will continue to draw us into challenging situations until it is released/forgiven, especially if we "sleep on it." This is the reason childhood trauma continues to play out in our lives, but this technique clears the clutter, allowing our true Self to emerge.

The following quote is from an attendee at one of our Heart Innergy workshops where we teach others how to use muscle testing to locate, and then clear, negative emotional patterns for themselves and others. This exercise then reprograms a more positive outcome.

"I have done several different techniques for emotional clearing, including EFT (Emotional Freedom Technique) and traditional counseling, but have found the NOW Points technique to be the quickest and most effective technique I have tried so far. It really clears effectively and easily. I just recently used it and, although it had several levels to clear, it worked exceptionally well."
— J.M. Springfield, MO

NOW Points Technique

Use the NOW Points when under mental or emotional stress:

- Feeling under pressure
- Having an argument with someone
- Alleviating fears and phobias
- Reducing physical or emotional trauma
- When life throws you a curve
- Works great on nightmares
- When you feel tired—focus on the feeling
- When you are in pain—focus on the pain

Location and Application

These are acupressure points that are the two slight bumps, located on the forehead, one or two inches above each eye. Place the index and middle finger, of each hand, on these points and push up slightly with almost no pressure; relax and breathe deeply.

Recall a past or present memory that is emotionally painful for you—"fight or flight mode." Lightly touch the NOW Points as you replay the stressful situation over and over in your mind, from beginning to end, as if it were on a movie screen or tape recording. Continue doing this as long as it takes for the memory to fade and you can no longer focus on it. Don't try to change the story, but feel it as if it were happening "NOW." To give it added release-power, you can ask a friend to hold these points for you—they do not even have to know your challenging issue.

You have begun to defuse the emotional feeling you are holding around the issue and have taken yourself out of the stressful "fight or flight mode," where it is hard to think clearly. You may have to defuse the same situation several times before you are totally free of the negative emotional energy charge. After using these points, when you think of the stressor, you will begin to notice that you feel lighter, as if a load has been lifted off your shoulders and indeed, it has!

Depending on the level of stress in the situation, you can hold the points for thirty seconds or as long as ten minutes, until you can no longer focus on the problem. You will find that when a similar circumstance again comes up in your life, you will react less and less, or not at all.

If you find yourself still reacting emotionally, use this as a barometer to let you know if further defusing needs to be done. Stay with the process and, eventually, you will feel a great freedom from the emotions that held you captive and your energy level will go up. *Caution:* Do not use this with extremely traumatic experiences without the help of a professional health care provider.

As mentioned before, this technique played a major role in helping me free myself from the habit/pattern of jealousy. Brenda also used this technique to help her through her divorce which was a perfect experience to teach her this technique. She was amazed at how easily and quickly this helped her stay emotionally balanced.

If the NOW Point technique peaks your interest, an excellent lay-person's book is, *Energy Medicine* by Donna Eden, who also had been a Touch for Health instructor. In her book, she gives a good example of helping someone overcome their fear of riding elevators by holding their NOW Points. I have found the same results as Eden, in using these points.

These points neutralize the body's flight response so that the person no longer reacts in their old habit patterns and fears. This causes the person to relax. They will notice a shift in their reactions the next time they are faced with the fearful situation.

This technique may have to be repeated several times when a reactive pattern appears in your life events. Coming from the voice of experience, I can say that it is well worth pursuing the inner peace that results from using the these points to help release old painful patterns.

A variation of this technique is to place one hand across your forehead and one hand behind your head. I use this hand position while holding these points on others. Try both ways to determine what works best for you.

A Good Reason to Defuse Anger

The Bible advises, "...do not let the sun go down while you are still angry...," (NIV Bible) which means don't go to bed angry. When you go to sleep, the negative emotional energy goes directly into the subconscious, adding to the clutter that is already there. When we use these points while bringing to mind a negative experience, we are accessing the subconscious memories and feelings, which bring them into the present moment where our full-focused attention will dissipate or change the energy.

We are the light of the world and we can use that light, which is our unconditional love, to balance our karmic debts from the subconscious mind, thus, bringing in more light.

Transforming the Situation—It's Only a Thought Away!

After you have used the NOW Points on a challenging situation, you can revise it. *Continue holding the points* and revise the challenging situation in your mind as you would have liked for it to have happen. This defuses the old pattern and infuse the new one.

For example, if you have an argument with someone and you want to change how you feel about it, hold the NOW Points to release the negative emotions around the situation. Then, in your mind, go back through the situation again and revise it into a more positive light—one that never seeks control over another person. Really feel the emotions of the positive outcome.

Another example; if you have difficulty standing up for yourself, then imagine the same situation and being able to do so. You can even use this to rewrite a bad dream, and when you do, notice how much better you feel about the dream when you recall it.

Your life rearranges itself to accommodate your belief system and the NOW Points can help with the rearranging process.

Meditation—How to get out of your mind without losing it

B ♫ Research scientist, Dr. Candace Pert, explains in her book, *Molecules of Emotions*, that meditation is one of the easiest, quickest, shortest, and cheapest ways to feeling good.

Meditation is used in a variety of ways. For some, it is a conscious attempt to become centered with their inner potential or creative nature. For others, it is a moment of perfect peace and serenity, recharging their batteries for a new day. Those for whom meditation has a spiritual connotation, it can be a means of connecting to the guidance of the Inner Presence, while others use it to visualize the goals they set for the day.

Meditation helps us to make the shift from the "wrong mind" (the ego personality) to the "Right Mind" (Divine Mind). The "wrong mind" has a strong hypnotic pull, using thoughts of fear, anger, worry, and self-doubt as its primary focus. This discipline is like a golden key that opens the door to the kingdom within. As *A Course in Miracles* says, *"I will be still [the mind] an instant and go home."*

Fortunately, today the ancient Eastern tradition of meditation is finally taking hold in the Western world as more people search for ways to reduce stress and anxiety, clear their minds, and find inner peace.

Eastern philosophy explains that all things proceed from a quiet mind. In much of the Western world, left-brained intellect is greatly treasured. Because of this, we have taken "over-thinking" to an addictive level—the mind then becomes like a run-away-train. Where's the Balance?

Ponderism: *Could it be that the quieter we become the more we hear, and that all questions are answered when we silently wait for the answers?*

Mental Detox Therapy

Meditation is to the mind what detoxifying is to the body. It literally cleans your mind of toxic waste created by years of negative thoughts—the *rotor-rooter of the subconscious mind*.

Even the Bible mentions that you would be transformed by the *renewing of your mind* and then you would be able to discern God's perfect will. Toxins come about from too much verbal and mental chatter, and the continual "white noise" of our daily lives. A focused and quiet mind is a spiritual treasure.

In prayer we are talking to God, and we might look at meditation as a way of listening for God's response. I believe that meditation is indirectly mentioned in the Bible: *"Be still and know that I am God."* When the external mind is quiet, all will be revealed.

In his book, *Stillness Speaks,* Eckhart Tolle, says that your inner essence, the truth of who you are, cannot be separated from stillness. Tolle refers to this inner essence as your I AM presence that goes much deeper than form.

I learned the value of meditation from the Edgar Cayce material in the 1970's, but years later had fallen back into the old habit of thinking I didn't have enough time, thus the "chatter box" mind took over. Because of several waking-dreams, experiences, and a deep inner knowing, I went back to the discipline that meditation requires and found it was the answer to my prayers. I had forgotten how "peace of mind" felt—my true home.

After only a few months, I stopped feeling overwhelmed by my schedule. I felt a greater connection with my intuition—my "right mind." In the face of challenges, my ego/personality mind quit taking over with anger, defensiveness, and best of all, I didn't lose any sleep by the mind wanting to "chew on it."

Benefits of Meditation

Feeling Good From the Inside Out
Go Within and You Won't Be Without!

- Improves concentration and increases your energy level—excessive thinking takes energy
- Connects with your inspirational, creative nature to be able to access a spiritual solution for every problem
- Relaxes the body deeper than sleep, allowing the activation of the body's own innate healing ability which is a boost to the immune system
- Restores harmony, peace, and clarity of mind, allowing greater self-confidence/self-love

Universal Principles for Meditation

In meditation the forms may vary, but certain principles are universal:

- *A quiet place*—Create a quiet place for uninterrupted time. Disconnect the telephone. Use earplugs if necessary.
- *A consistent routine*—Choose the same time and place for daily meditation.
- *A comfortable position*—A straight-backed chair may be helpful; hold the spine comfortably erect.
- *A focused mind—Focus on a word, thought, symbol, or your breath.* This helps keeps the mental chatter out of the way.
- *A routine of practice*—Be consistent! This is more important than duration. Even one minute of meditation has benefits and as you begin to feel the calming results you will find time to do it.

For a few years, I had gotten away from the disciplined practice of quieting the mind, so when I first started the basic focused-breathing exercise, my undisciplined mental chatter kept interfering. It took a couple of weeks before it became quiet. Consistency, structure, patience, and persistence are keys to meditation. Also certain foods, emotional stress (if someone just gave you *a piece of their mind*), and caffeine hinders the process.

Breath Workout—Conscious Breathing—the Breath of Life

The one thing that we can always control in the face of any uncomfortable situation is our breathing. By focusing on our breathing, we bring our mind into the present moment. Because breath is formless, whenever you focus on your breathing you are absolutely in the present moment and connected with your intuition.

If you will practice focusing on your breath at random times throughout the day, you will become aware of the stillness therein. Then, when under stress, it will be easier to remember to do this exercise, which will help calm a *stress-full* moment.

Deep breathing can be done at anytime, anywhere, preventing and relieving harmful reactions of stress to the body. Shallow breathing is a result of tension and creates an oxygen shortage to the brain. Less oxygen to the brain actually activates the "chatter box" mind. This can hinder the ability to think clearly and to concentrate, not to mention harming the physical body.

Yogi Ramacharaka, in his book, *Science of Breath*, explains that in the air we breathe is a substance (not oxygen) containing all vitality, and from which life was derived. This substance, called *Prana*, is a Sanskrit word meaning "Absolute Energy;" it can penetrate where oxygen cannot. Oxygen is used by the circulatory system, while prana is used by the nervous system. Prana radiates vitality in strengthening all parts of the body, including the brain.

Our continual thinking, willing, and acting, exhausts our supply of prana. It is used up by the nervous system and thus, a constant replenishing is necessary. The greater portion of prana we acquire comes from the air we breathe; thus the importance of proper breathing!

The Bible also mentions that God is the Father of heavenly light. Could it be that, when the Bible mentions light it is referring to prana? Was this prana/light what the Master Jesus meant when he said that we are the "light of the world," meaning it is in each one of us? Later in this chapter, Linda gives a wonderful white-light technique to help you have a personal experience with the healing power of this light.

Meditation Exercises

Conscious Breathing Exercise

Practice time: three to ten minutes a day, or longer.

1. Focus on your breathing as it moves in and out of your body.
2. Feel your abdomen expanding and contracting slightly as you breathe into the body, with each inhalation and exhalation.
3. If the mind wanders; it most likely will at first, just gently but firmly bring it back to focus on the breath.
4. Repeat a sound, a phrase, or a verse from a prayer in conjunction with breathing.

We have found Eckhart Tolle's book, *Stillness Speaks,* to be an excellent meditation/ponderism book in addition to using phrases from *A Course In Miracles* and your *Bible,* etc. Your meditation can simply be a prayer of gratitude/appreciation for your blessings. Before going to sleep each night, spend from three to five minutes focusing on the blessings in your day. Do this for thirty days and watch your attitude and thus your life change.

Take a Mini-Mind Vacation

Many people are under the misperception that you have to spend a lot of time meditating, but this is not so. You can even grab one to two minutes of mental quiet time by focusing on your breath at a stop light—a mini-mind vacation. Just stopping during your day for 2-3 minutes will make a difference in your stress level. Your life can become a continual meditation; keeping you from feeling overwhelmed by a busy schedule.

Walking Meditation

Walk slowly and deliberately to and from your car when at work, shopping, or other activity. Pay attention to the basic movements in each step. As you walk, focus on taking slow, deep breaths and how it feels when each foot takes a step. This practice teaches you to slow down, be fully present, and can ease the transition between home and work, especially after a hectic day.

Give it a Rest! (the mind)

Any activity that is done by habit and does not require thinking, is great to use with this technique: walking up and down stairs, washing your hands, tending a garden, etc. Be fully present with whatever you are doing and pay attention to the sensory perceptions related to the activity. If it is washing your hands, notice how the water feels on your hands, the sound of the water, and even how the drying towel feels.

Create Your Own Mini-Mind Vacation

Be persistent in letting your mind know that you are serious about having less stress and more inner peace in your life. Get creative by finding your own mini-mind vacation opportunities. A good example; each time you get into your car, pause for a few seconds in silence. Take a few deep breaths imaging any stress leaving the body. As a reminder to make this a habit, you might put up a sticky note.

Living From the Heart Meditation

In the morning just as you begin to have conscious awareness of waking up, focus your attention on the area of your heart center and stay there in silence. Do not look at the clock, or allow the mind to begin thinking about the day, just remain in that silent stillness for a few minutes.

When you feel stable in the heart center, this will only take a minute or so, begin to think about positive charged words: appreciation, joy, gratitude, beauty, harmony—any positive words you feel drawn to focus on.

If done correctly, this will change the entire quality or tone for your day. We all have experienced those days when we wake up late and begin the day rushing, and then the whole day seems rushed or out of sync.

Once you do this meditation for a while, you will notice that just by placing your attention on the heart area you will be able to recall this *heart feeling* anytime during the day that you feel stress and need a mini-vacation.

Just before going to sleep at night let it be known to your inner guidance, the soul, that you would like to become more aware of learning how to "Live from the Heart." Pay attention to any dreams and waking dreams.

White Light Meditation

L ♫ This can be very helpful at anytime, especially doing it the last thing at night before falling asleep or the first thing in the morning before getting up. This need only take a few seconds, but it can help bring every cell of your body into the present moment. If I awaken feeling anxious about something, I hold the NOW Points while doing this exercise. You will be surprised how much better you will feel.

This is also a powerful, self-healing meditation when you feel the need to boost the immune system. The energy of the white light is prana, the life force energy discussed earlier. It is very effective when you feel the first symptoms of an illness, but can also be used if you already have a physical illness. When used at frequent intervals and with intense focus, you should see results fairly soon.

- Sit comfortably or lie flat on your back; close your eyes.
- Begin by imagining a ball of brilliant white light, increasing in intensity, below your feet.
- Slowly bring the ball of light up through your body a few inches at a time, pausing about fifteen seconds, or until you get the nudge to move on.
- Slowly move up your body, with as much intensity as you can, making the ball brighter and brighter as you go.
- Once you reach the top of your head, let your attention run back through the body like a wave, a few times, from feet to head and back again taking only a minute or so.
- This can be repeated many times until you feel a shift in the way you feel—the more intensely you can do this, the more dramatic the change.
- Be creative with this exercise; focus on a spiritual word while doing the exercise, or change the color and/or the size of the light.

I used this meditation on a camping trip when I felt feverish and decided to try this technique before taking medication. It relieved my fever quickly.

B ♫ I too have used this with wonderful results, especially at the onset of a sore throat or cold and cuts in half the time it takes to recover. I can actually feel my physical body responding to the energy as it moves over certain areas. I always feel more energy after doing this meditation.

The Unity Breath Meditation
—Unity With Mother Earth, Father Sky

This meditation is from the book, *Living in the Heart* by Drunvalo Melchizedek. He received it from an inner teacher, Sri Yukteswar, during a meditation and received these words;

> *"God is always everywhere, but humans do not always perceive God. The Unity Breath meditation takes you directly, consciously into God's presence."*

Drunvalo works with the indigenous peoples on the Earth especially the Mayan and Hopi Indians. Drunvalo says, *"One thing that indigenous peoples of the world have taught me is that before any important ceremony, one must connect in love with Mother Earth, then with Father Sky and through this experience ultimately with Great Spirit, or God."*

Through several dreams and waking dreams, we were guided to attend Drunvalo's workshop, in the spring of 2009, where he graciously gave us permission to use this meditation in our book. We found his genuineness to be very refreshing and the meditation to be very powerful. Follow your heart and let it tell you if this meditation is for you.

The Unity Breath

To begin this meditation, relax by following your breathing for a few moments. When it feels right, begin the Unity Breath meditation.

Unity with the Divine Mother (Mother Earth)

- Place your attention, with as much detail as you can, on a place in nature that you feel is the most beautiful place you can think of. Use whatever means of seeing or sensing this beautiful place. We all have our own way to perceive this whether it is visual, audio, or feeling. Begin to feel the love for this place and for all of nature. Continue with this feeling of love until your heart is beating with the warmth of your love. Let this feeling of love grow in your heart and begin to feel it in your whole body.

- When the time feels right, send your love to the center of the Earth using your intention so that Mother Earth can directly feel the love you have for her. You can place your love into a small sphere to contain it and send it to the Mother if you wish, but it is your intention that is important. Then wait, as a child. Wait until Mother Earth sends her love back to you and you can feel it. You are her child, and she loves you.

- When you feel this love return from Mother Earth, let it enter your energy body and permeate the cells in your body by allowing it to move any way and to any place in your body. Just allow. Feel the flow of love between you and Mother Earth. Stay in this union of love that surrounds you as long as you wish.

Unity with the Divine Father (Father Sky)

- "At the right moment, which only you can know, without breaking the love union with your Mother, look to your Father, to your Heavenly Father. Look to the rest of creation beyond the Earth. Place your attention on a night sky. See the Milky Way as it meanders across the heavens. Watch the Planets and the Moon swirl around you and the Earth. Feel the Sun hidden beneath the Earth. Realize the incredible depth of space."

- "Feel the love you have for the Father, for the Divine Father is the spirit of all of creation, except the Divine Mother. And when this love becomes so great that it just can't stay inside you any longer, let it move into the heavens with your intention. Again, you can send your love into the heavens inside a small sphere, if you wish."

- "Once your love has been sent into the heavens to the Divine Father, again you wait; you wait for the Father to send his love back to you. And of course, he will always do so. You are his child forever, and the Divine Father will always, always love you. And just like with the Mother's love, when you feel the love of the Divine Father enter your being, let it move anywhere it wants to. It is your Father's love, and it is pure."

- "At this moment something that rarely happens is manifesting: the Holy

Trinity is alive on Earth. The Divine Mother and the Divine Father are joined with you in pure love and you, the Divine Child, complete the triangle." It is a sacred moment in its own right, so just be with your divine parents and feel the love.

- "And so the final step in this meditation is to become aware of the presence of God—all around you and within you." Spend time in this stillness moment and feel God's love caress and nurture you.

Additional Techniques

Stillness Messages

—When Startling News Threatens Your Peace

B ♫ When we hear any news that is "difficult to digest," our conscious mind will click out for a few seconds, which is all that is needed to clearly hear our intuitive guidance. Anytime you hear sudden, disturbing news, stop immediately and ask within: What do I do now?

I have used this technique several times in my life with excellent results that provided clear and accurate messages of guidance. There were times I questioned the information but it always proved to be accurate, I just had to stay out of the way by not listening to the mental chatter full of self-doubt.

One example happened many years ago when leaving my place of employment, in a very influential section of town, I realized that my car had been stolen. Fortunately, I remembered to stop and ask (within) what I should do. The calm inner voice said, "Let it go." As I did this, there was an actual physical sensation of energy leaving my body—a peculiar feeling.

As I worked to maintain my emotional balance, I could see Spirit's guiding hand. When the police found my car several days later, it had been wrecked and totaled. There were many synchronistic events in getting a new car, some of which I wouldn't understand until much later. After my divorce, financially I wouldn't have been able to get a new car and the blessing was that I always had dependable transportation and somehow the car payment was always made-—on time!

Twilight Messages—Twice a Day, "Out-of-Mind Moments"

B ♫ During the delicate moments of going to sleep or waking, we are in the twilight gap of shifting from waking/thinking to sleeping/unconscious. In these *out-of-mind moments*, we have an opportunity to communicate directly with our intuitive guidance. In this gap, the *white noise* of our personality-mind is asleep, allowing a doorway to the celestial realm to open.

My awareness of this process occurred after reading the non-fiction book, *Out of My Mind,* from one of my favorite authors, Richard Bach. Bach knew that if he focused intensely enough on any mechanical problem with his airplane, he would get a solution during this twilight state.

Some years later, upon awakening I was nudged to ask, "What does Divine Spirit want me to ponder today?" I was startled by a quick reply, *"Love Yourself To Death."* I didn't know what this meant and my first thought was—is this going to hurt, and I'm not ready to die just yet.

Pondering this message helped me to realize that to *Love Yourself To Death* is actually *Loving Yourself into Life.* This valuable insightful message became on of my spiritual articles. Please go to, www.bloggingwithgod.com to view the whole story.

Open Book Technique

This is one of our favorite techniques to get instant help. You can use any book that you are intuitively drawn to—we have even used the phone book. Whenever a challenging situation arises or you just want confirmation for a decision, this offers quick access to a solution—right at your fingertips.

All that is needed is to quiet your mind, say a prayer for help, feel gratitude for the answer you will receive and then, randomly, open the book. Without looking, place your finger, intuitively, on a page (or simply let your eyes be drawn to a place on the page). This is your message, and it is significant when placed within the context of your situation.

* * *

True to Form—Brenda Wraps It Up

I guess it shouldn't have been a surprise that I woke up at 5:00 a.m. the morning of the day we were to complete this chapter, and the book, with a clear direction for the ending and a couple of things we had forgotten to add.

As usual, Linda had written the first part of the chapter with my occasional inserts, and now it was my turn to finish the chapter and the book.

Humorously, Linda had no anxiety about having to finish the book because she knew it was my job. When she Skyped me to start our writing session, I told her the final words had just been e-mailed to her. Our "Twin Radar" was functioning well.

When All Else Fails, Hold Hands and Pray

In January of 2006, I received a vivid dream and the feeling or tone of the dream told me it was important for the times in which we are living. My early-morning guidance was that sharing this dream would be a perfect way to end this chapter on *Putting Your Spiritual House in Order.*

In the dream, I was with a group of people, and we saw strange lights in the sky, like an odd electrical storm—it seemed like something out of a Sci-fi movie. We wondered if it was the end of the world, as this strange event was certainly out of our control. Instantly, I knew that *we all needed to hold hands and pray,* then we would be okay and at peace. It was then important that our group split up into four groups and go tell others not to be afraid, but to hold hands and pray and they would be okay.

I got a confirmation on the importance of this dream while visiting Linda and sharing it with her. With a surprised look on her face, she immediately got a spiritual book she was reading and explained that she had just read a section that was very similar to my dream.

The passage in the book was about a turbulent sky and the importance of keeping still, staying out of fear, and praying. We both felt shivers down our spines, which was our confirmation for truth, and felt that we were being given important information for the times ahead.

Not until January of 2007 did I know, fully, what this dream meant. We were having an ice storm unlike anything we had ever experienced; it was so bad that it was on the national news and many were without power for weeks. I will never forget that Friday evening, about midnight—it still brings tears to my eyes as I write this and recall hearing my beautiful trees cracking and falling from the weight of the ice. In the stillness of the night, I could also hear the horrible distant sounds of neighboring trees crashing down too.

I knew my prayer for the "tree angels" to hold up the limbs wasn't going to happen. Inwardly, I prayed, asking for direction. My mind, not having a clue on how to handle this situation, was thankfully out of the way; one of those rare "out of mind moments." The answer was clear, as the above dream came to mind, and this was one of those times to hold hands and pray.

As I surrendered to, "what is, is" and prayed, a peaceful calm came over me. I asked Spirit what to pray for, as my prayer to save the trees wasn't going to happen. A clear voice inside my mind said only one word—"Grace." For me, grace is given when I have exhausted all avenues to resolve a situation and at that point of total surrender (call/prayer for help), Divine Grace/help is given. With tears, I let my trees go; not my will but Yours be done.

I now knew what the dream meant, and what I had to do. I didn't have to be with anyone physically, as in prayer our hearts would join, instantly, through our intentions. I visualized holding hands with all of my wonderful, heart-buddy friends in a huge circle surrounding the city, as I knew they would be praying too.

The grace of God was with us as I saw many blessings come out of this challenging experience. Inwardly I was reminded that this was Mother Nature's way of a good pruning and sure enough two years later the trees were beautiful and revitalized with new growth. We now have an organic garden that replaced two of our fallen trees.

If you follow your heart, then, when everything in life seems to be crashing down around you, rest assured that when you, "hold hands and pray for grace," *the peace of God that surpasses all understanding will be your guide*. Then,

Grace will be given to open your heart
and show you the way!

What you have read here is
THE LIVING CODE,
the journey doesn't end here!
As a living code the path is like living waters,
a stream, alive and eternally flowing.

For our "Blogging With God" articles,
go to:
www.bloggingwithgod.com

As mentioned in Chapter 5, we would love
to have your waking dream stories.
Please e-mail or write
and as a group we will continue
THE LIVING CODE STREAM.

Check for updates at:
www.thelivingcode.com

Selected Bibliography

A Course In Miracles 2nd rev. ed., Mill Valley, CA: Foundation for Inner Peace, 1993, www.acim.org

Andrews, Ted. *Animal-Speak, The Spiritual & Magical Powers of Creatures Great & Small*. St. Paul, MN: Llewellyn Worldwide, 1994

Bach, Richard. *Messiah's Handbook: Reminders for the Advanced Soul*. Charlottesville, VA: Hampton Roads Publishing Co., Inc., 2004

Byrne, Rhonda. *The Secret*. Hillsboro, OR: Beyond Words, 2006

Babylon 5. DVD. Burbank, CA: Warner Bros. Entertainment Inc., 2004

Café, Sônia. *Angel Meditations,* 64 illustrated cards, Illustrations by Neide Innecco, Stamford, CT: U.S. Games Systems, Inc., 1996

Curtis, Donald. *Your Thoughts Can Change your Life*. New York, NY: Warner Book Co., 1975

Dyer, Wayne W., Ph.D. *10 Secrets for Success and Inner Peace*, Carlsbad, CA: Hay House 2001

Eden, Donna. *Energy Medicine*, New York: Penguin Putnam Inc., 1999

Gray, John. *Men are from Mars, Women are from Venus*. New York: Harper Collins Publisher, Inc., 1992

Grof, Christina and Stanislav, M.D. *Spiritual Emergency: When Personal Transformation becomes a Crisis*. New York, NY: G. P. Putnam's Sons, 1989

Groundhog Day. DVD. Culver City, CA: Columbia Pictures Industries, Inc., 1993

Hay, Louise L. *Heal Your Body*. Carlsbad, CA: Hay House, Inc., 2003

Hicks, Esther and Jerry: *The Teachings of Abraham*™ The Law of Attraction in Action Workshop, DVD, III, Carlsbad, CA: Hay House, Inc., 2008

Hicks, Esther and Jerry: *The Teachings of Abraham*™. Abraham-Hicks Publications CD 4/02/08: Fort Lauderdale, FL

Holy Bible New International Version

Holy Bible King James Version

Javane, Faith and Bunker, Dusty. *Numerology and the Divine Triangle*. Ataglen, PA: Whitford Press, 1979

Katie, Byron. *Loving What Is*, New York: Three Rivers Press, 2002

Lappin, Dave. *Dream Logic – Waking Up to the World of Dreams*. Springfield, MO: e-Book, Self-published 2008 website www.understand-your-dreams.com

Levine, Barbara Hoberman. *Your Body Believes Every Word You Say:* The Language of the Body/Mind Connection. Santa Rosa, CA: Aslan Publishing, 1991

Linn, Denise. *The Secret Language of Signs*. New York: Ballantine Books, 1996

Lipton, Bruce. *The Biology of Belief: Unleashing The Power Of Consciousness, Matter And Miracles*. San Antonio, TX: Mountain of LoveTM Books, 2005

Melchizedek, Drunvalo. *Living in the Heart*. Flagstaff, AZ: Light Technology Publishing, 2003

Parrish-Harra, Carol E. Ph.D. *The New Dictionary of Spiritual Thought*. Tahlequah, OK: Sparrow Hawk Press, 2002

Pert, Candace B., *Molecules of Emotion*, Ph.D. New York: Simon & Schuster, 2003

Ponder, Catherine. *Open Your Mind to Prosperity*. Unity Village, MO: Unity Books, 1971

Rain, Mary Summer. *In Your Dreams: The Ultimate Dream Dictionary*. Charlottesville, VA: Hampton Roads Publishing Co., Inc., 2004

Ramacharaka, Yogi. *Science of Breath: A Complete Manual of The Oriental Breathing Philosophy*. Chicago, IL: The Yogi Publication Society, 1905

Redfield, James. *The Celestine Prophecy* . New York: Warner Books, Inc., 1993

Renard, Gary. *The Disappearance of the Universe*. Berkeley, CA: Fearless Books, 2003

Sams, Jamie & Carson, David. *Medicine Cards: The Discovery of Power Through the Ways of Animals*. Santa Fe, NM: Bear & Company, 1988

Sugrue, Thomas. *There is a River: The Story of Edgar Cayce*. Virginia Beach, VA: A.R.E. Press, 1942

Sechrist, Elsie. *Dreams: Your Magic Mirror: With Interpretations of Edgar Cayce*. Virginia Beach, VA: Association of Research & Enlightenment Press, 1995

Touch for Health Kinesiology. www.touch4health.com

Tolle, Eckhart. *Stillness Speaks*. Vancouver, Canada: Namaste Publishing, 2003

Tolle, Eckhart. *The Power of Now*. Novato, CA: New World Library, 1999

Tolle, Eckhart. *Practicing the Power of Now*, Essential Teachings, Meditations, and Exercises From *The Power of Now*. Novato, CA: New World Library, 1999

Tolle, Eckhart. *A New Earth: Awakening to Your Life's Purpose*. New York: Dutton a Penguin Group (USA), Inc., 2005

Trigueirinho, (Book listing on next page)

Virtue, Doreen Ph.D. *Healing With The Angels*. Carlsbad, CA: Hay House, Inc., 1999

Walsch, Neale Donald. *I believe God wants you to know:* Daily Inspirational http://www.nealedonaldwalsch.com/

Wapnick, Kenneth. *The 50 Miracle Principles of A Course in Miracles*, Crompond, NY: Foundation for "A Course in Miracles" 1987, www.facim.org

Wattles, Wallace D. *The Science of Getting Rich and the Science of Being Great*. Lakemont, GA: CSA Press, 1910 (get a free download of this book: www.whitedovebooks.co.uk/newsletter/science-download-page)

What the Bleep Do we Know!?, DVD. Beverly Hills, CA: Twentieth Century Fox Home Entertainment, Inc., 2004

José Trigueirinho Netto
Brazilin Philosopher

Check the website for a list of Trigueirinho's CD's
translated into English.
www.callinghumanity.org

Books by Trigueirinho in English

Beyond Karma. Minas Gerais, Brazil: Irdin Editora, 1996

Calling Humanity: A Cosmic Event is Taking Place, Information for the New Time. Minas Gerais, Brazil: Irdin Editora, 2002

The Mystery of the Cross in the Present Planetary Transition. Minas Gerais, Brazil: Irdin Editora, 2003

Niskalkat. Minas Gerais, Brazil: Irdin Editora, 1993

Noah's Vessel. Minas Gerais, Brazil: Irdin Editora, 1990

The Voice of Amhaj. Minas Gerais, Brazil: Irdin Editora, 1993 (Amhaj is Master El Morya)

The Pocket Book Series

The Light Within You
Doorway to A Kingdom
We Are Not Alone
Winds of Spirit
Finding the Temple
There is Peace
Path Without Shadows

About the Authors

The Twins
—*become like little children to enter
the kingdom of heaven.*

About Brenda

Brenda lives with her husband, Dave, in Missouri. She is an ordained interfaith minister and a spiritual writer of *Ponderisms—Potent Points To Ponder, Spiritual Insights for Daily Living*. These Ponderisms can be found at the web site: www.bloggingwithgod.com.

Brenda has been a certified instructor and practitioner of the energy therapy systems of Reiki since 1997 and Quantum-Touch® since 2006. Information at: www.reikimissouri.com or www.quantumtouchmissouri.com.

She has been a certified past life regressionist since 1996 and created a course to begin teaching in 1998. In 2002 she was certified as an Advanced Past Life Regressionist from the international author and lecturer Dolores Cannon.

She is an intuitive artist and instructor of Heart Portal Soul Paintings—www.heartportalpaintings.com. She has also taught classes in numerology, intuitive development and muscle testing. She and Dave teach a workshop: Dreams and Waking Dreams—The Science of Spiritual Communication.

Her hobbies include, tending to her vegetable, herb and flower gardens and nature walks to satisfy her addiction as a "tree hugger." Her corporate background is in property management, leasing and bookkeeping.

About Linda

Linda lives with her husband, Tom, in Arkansas with their two dogs and one cat. She is an ordained interfaith minister, and in 1998 graduated from Sancta Sophia Seminary in Tahlequah, Oklahoma with a certification in spiritual healing and pastoral counseling.

She has studied energy healing since the early 90's when she became a "Touch for Health (TFH) Kinesiology" (muscle response testing) instructor and practitioner with a focus on pain relief and spiritual/emotional healing. In the early 90's, she developed a style of spiritual/emotional healing she and Brenda now teach—"Heart INNER-gy Techniques (HIT) Workshop." She no longer teaches TFH as her primary focus is on spiritual writing and giving workshops about spiritual/emotional healing.

In 2006 she became a Certified Quantum-Touch® practitioner and instructor. She has incorporated Quantum-Touch® with the HIT system to teach others how to free themselves from addictive emotional patterns.

As a hobby, she enjoys her organic garden which turned out to be a great blessing after a day of working on the computer. For many years she owned a successful alteration shop which allowed her time to teach and write, and currently has a successful multi-level marketing business.

The Twins are currently co-writing spiritual articles you can view at
their web site: www.bloggingwithgod.com.
A collection of these articles will be incorporated into
a future book: *Blogging With God—Everyone Can Do It!*

**The Twins are available for lectures and workshops.
Sponsors, please contact us through our web page:
www.thelivingcode.com**

THE LIVING CODE
Experiential Workshop
—The first aid kit for challenging times.

With Linda and Brenda McCoy

"The twins" are here to assist you on your journey to self-discovery/ self-knowledge with their down-to-earth, common sense approach to addressing life's challenges.

This vital information gives you exercises for a permanent direct connection with the Soul's wisdom which helps you to make better life choices. This Soul connection helps tremendously in understanding and de-stressing during life's challenges.

You will enjoy "the twins" contagious zest for life as they share inspirational stories, practical guidance and humorous insights.

In this workshop learn and experience:

- Effective techniques for handling day-to-day stress.
- Exercises to renew your sense of enthusiasm and inspiration for life's journey and recognize your purpose in life.
- How to become spiritually bilingual—learn Soul's language.
- How to take your intuitive abilities to a new level.
- The difference between creating from the mind versus creating from the heart and why this is so important.
- How to acknowledge, understand and clear karmic patterns.
- How to move past fears and self-doubts.
- How to create and maintain "the perfect relationship."
- A guided meditation to help you connect with your angels and understand how the past is affecting your life.
- A renewed enthusiasm and inspiration for life's journey.
- The dynamics of the group energy with like minded people.

If you would like to sponsor a workshop, see our web site.

For more information: www.thelivingcode.com

— ORDER FORM —

THE LIVING CODE

	Quantity	Total
$15.95 US	_____	.... _____
Shipping	....	$3.00
($1.00 for each additional)		_____
Total Amount .... $		_____

(Sales tax included where applicable.)

Check or money order payable to:

Twin Heart Productions
P.O. Box 3182
Springfield, MO 65808

Also order at: www.thelivingcode.com using PayPal

Even if you do not have a PayPal account
you can still use your Visa or Master Card

Shipping & Mailing Address
(Please Print)

Name: _____

Address: _____

City: _____State:_____Zip _____

E-mail: _____

Phone: _____   CREDIT CARD   VISA * MC
(for shipping / billing questions only)

Name on card: _____cvv_____

Credit Card # _____EXP DATE _____

Notes

Notes

LaVergne, TN USA
13 December 2009
166851LV00004B/8/P

9 780984 283903